SEVEN ON BLACK

Seven on Black

Reflections on
the Negro Experience
in America

EDITED BY

William G. Shade

AND

Roy C. Herrenkohl

J. B. Lippincott Company

PHILADELPHIA/NEW YORK

To Ellen and Lou

We are here, *and here we are likely to be. To imagine that we shall ever be eradicated is absurd and ridiculous. We can be remodified, changed, and assimilated, but never extinguished. We repeat, therefore that* **we are here;** *and that this is* our *country. . . . We shall neither die out, nor be driven out; but shall go with this people, either as a testimony against them, or as an evidence in their favor throughout their generations.*

—Frederick Douglass

Preface

The essays in this volume were first delivered as lectures in a series at Lehigh University in the fall of 1968. A visit to the campus the previous April by James Farmer, just three days after the murder of the Reverend Martin Luther King, served to coalesce student interest in the "Negro experience in America." Although the series was organized by the editors of this volume, it would not have succeeded without the support of the Lehigh students who provided the funds for the series through the Forum for Visiting Lecturers and the Class of 1969 and who faithfully attended the Monday night lectures. The editors would like to thank particularly Charles I. Cogut, Philip H. Gitlen, and Robert A. Strauss, who did much of the leg-work required in the presentation of the series. We would also like to thank our colleague Lawrence H. Leder, who has been a constant source of aid and support and who originally suggested the publication of these essays in book form.

Contents

SEVEN ON BLACK

Introduction

Few persons doubt that a realistic re-examination of the historical relationship between the races in the United States is essential to understand our present racial crisis. This means not only examining white attitudes toward blacks, but also the nature and scope of the black experience in white America.

Afro-Americans have been one of the major hyphenate groups in America since the eighteenth century, when blacks actually made up a greater proportion of the population, even in such Northern cities as Boston and New York, than they do today. Yet most white historians have ignored the black subculture, except when attitudes toward it became points of contention within the white majority. Only when dealing with the Civil War and Reconstruction have white historians placed blacks anywhere near the center of the historical stage, and then more often as scenery than as actors.

The generation of white historians writing before 1920 generally recognized the importance of slavery as a causative factor in bringing on the Civil War, but they presented black men as inferior beings fit only for the most menial tasks even when free. Although hostile to the institution of slavery, the leading historian of the day, James Ford Rhodes, was sympathetic to the plight of the white slaveholder. He believed that "modern science" had proved the black distinctly inferior to the white and bitterly opposed the efforts of the Radical Republicans during Reconstruction. Ulrich B. Phillips, the foremost student of slavery during these years, relied heavily on the records of large plantation owners and tended to view the institution through their eyes as a system for the social control of an inferior race. William A. Dunning and his students accepted this view and joined Rhodes in attacking the efforts at postwar reconstruction as corrupt and unrealistic. Explaining the abandonment of Reconstruction, Dunning reveals his generation's evaluation of the black man:

Gradually there emerged again the idea of Jefferson and Clay and Lincoln, which had been hooted and hissed into obscurity during the prevalence of abolitionist fever. This was that the ultimate root of the trouble in the South had been, not the institution of slavery, but the coexistence in one society of two races so distinct in characteristics as to render coalescence impossible, that slavery had been a *modus vivendi* through which social life was possible; and that after its disappearance, its place must be taken by some set of conditions which if more humane and beneficent in accidents, must in essence express the same fact of racial inequality. . . . It seems most improbable that the historian will soon, or ever, have to record a reversal of the conditions which this process has established.

The subsequent generation of historians writing between the World Wars altered these views slightly and made fewer references to the inferiority of the Negro race, but nonetheless pushed the black man farther out of the historical picture. Heavily influenced by Frederick Jackson Turner and Charles A. Beard, historians in the thirties and forties focused attention on the conflict between "industrialists" and "agrarians." Howard K. Beale criticized the abolitionists as impractical fanatics who "knew nothing of the Southern negro, but devoutly believed in their own theories," and the Radical Republicans as hypocritical corruptionists who used humanitarian "claptrap" to hide their malevolent design of business domination. According to E. Merton Coulter, another white historian writing during these years:

Radical Reconstruction was doomed to fail. With a crass, materialistic design it was cloaked in a garb of high idealistic justice, but its rulers were inexperienced, ignorant and corrupt. They forgot what the world had learned and experienced during the preceding two thousand years. Millenniums and Utopias might be written about, but intelligent people knew that they were never to be realized in this life.

As their interpretation of the Civil War and Reconstruction reveals, this extremely influential generation of American historians, whose views are found in all but the most recent college textbooks, most often ignored the black man and emphasized conflicts between white economic groups. This is clear in their treatments of the periods of "reform," in which they describe the numerous "advances in democracy" without noting that these were often limited to whites and accompanied by further degradation of the black man.

That the nation's blacks were not touched by political advances is clear if one examines the impact of Jacksonian Democracy and Progressivism on the Negro in America. The Jacksonians not only supported Southern demands to curtail the right of petition and suppress freedom of speech on the slavery issue; they also led the movement to disfranchise free Northern Negroes and circumscribe their civil rights. It was, after all, Roger B. Taney, Jackson's confidant and henchman in the "bank war," who as Chief Justice of the United States delivered the opinion of the Court in the Dred Scott decision. He wrote there that for more than a century knowledgeable men had regarded Negroes as "beings of an inferior order, and altogether unfit to associate with the white race, either in social or political relations; and so far inferior, that they had no rights which the white man was bound to respect; . . ." The record of the Progressives was, if anything, worse. A few Progressives, usually with Socialist backgrounds or from old abolitionist families, joined the opposition to the deteriorating conditions of blacks after 1900, but in the main Progressive reforms were "for whites only." Southern Progressivism was practically indistinguishable from the move to deprive blacks of their civil rights. The significant number of Negroes who switched party allegiance to support Woodrow Wilson in 1912 saw their hopes quickly dashed. The scholar-President, who had referred to the freedmen as "a host of dusky children untimely put out of school" and praised the racist film *Birth of a Nation*, introduced segregation into the Federal departments, removed Negro office holders in the South, and acquiesced in the violently anti-Negro activities of many of his supporters. There was even an increase in lynching and racial violence during the Wilson years which must have given the slogan "The New Freedom" a rather hollow ring for black Americans.

Such contradictions have become increasingly apparent as students since World War II have begun extensive investigation of the history of black Americans. Writing in the *Journal of Negro History* in 1957, John Hope Franklin, a leading contemporary black historian, noted that writers of both races were producing a "new Negro history" and that for the first time there was "a striking resemblance between what historians are writing and what has actually happened in the history of the American Negro." The contemporary movement for racial justice, which C. Vann Woodward has called the "Second Reconstruction," has accelerated this development; and probing studies, not only of white attitudes toward Negroes, but also of the conditions of slavery, the internal development of the black community, and the thought of Negro leaders, have appeared in recent years, causing a re-evaluation of American history generally.

The seven essays in this book present several of the best

scholars of the current generation dealing with various aspects of the Afro-American experience, past and present. The initial essay analyzes the recent interest in the past of the black man. Four of the essays that follow are by historians and deal with the slave's response to slavery, white racial attitudes as a factor in the abandonment of Reconstruction, the economic views of Booker T. Washington, and the response of the Negro church to the urbanization process. The two final essays, by political scientists, analyze the dilemma facing black urban politicians and provide a context for a deeper understanding of the meaning of demands for Black Power. Each is an original essay published here for the first time. By presenting new research and introducing new concepts, these essays attempt to provide an imaginative starting point for further investigation of the black experience in the United States.

1.
OTEY M. SCRUGGS

Why Study Afro-American History?

In the first essay, Professor Otey M. Scruggs, of Syracuse University, addresses himself to the question which is fundamental to this volume. It is a subject that has been too often discussed in an atmosphere of racial hostility and mutual recrimination. Professor Scruggs's analysis of the multiple functions of the study of the black experience in the United States avoids extremist rhetoric and brings a sense of proportion to the subject. He properly shows that the scholarly study of the Afro-American past is neither a new nor a frivolous enterprise, although the present interest in the subject is clearly related to current problems. He dismisses the supposedly dangerous consequences of the search for black heroes and shows that American history is incomplete without consideration of the black experience. In doing so he does not deny that a fuller understanding of Afro-American history will heighten the blacks' feelings of integrity and identity. However, Professor Scruggs's main claim is that the study of Afro-American history will lead to a better and more accurate understanding of the entire American past: one infused with the tragic sense often lacking in the usual treatments and cleansed of the self-righteousness vividly present in the histories of only a decade ago.

WITHIN the past few years interest in Afro-American history has reached unprecedented heights. From a fringe subject Afro-American history has become the "latest glamour field." What lies behind this dramatic turnabout? First is the stepped-up drive among Afro-Americans in the 1960s for equal consideration, a "revolutionary" quest for dignity and recognition in a society that has always belittled black people when it has not ignored them. Second is the end of white western colonialism and the consequent rise of non-white states in Afro-Asia, reawakening among Afro-Americans dormant feelings of spiritual identification with Africa. Third is the compelling desire of such scholars as August Meier, Benjamin Quarles, and John Hope Franklin, reeling from the impact of a swiftly changing world, to reinterpret the American past in an effort to provide fresh meaning to the present as we proceed into the future. What emerges from consideration of these immense changes is the profound element of tragedy that reaches from the Afro-American past into the present. Might it not then be possible that a knowledge of Afro-American history would provide a useful corrective to that romantic optimism so deeply rooted in the American character?

The black revolution of our time has focused attention as never before on the tragic cleavage between black and white that has always existed in this country. Afro-Americans are now less concerned with being integrated into a society that remains more racist than it cares to admit, and more with establishing a consciousness of themselves as a unique group. As such, they are demanding a history that acknowledges not simply their presence but their humanity as well. Black people know, perhaps better than most, that an important aid in fostering group pride is an historical tradition that depicts their ancestors' involvement in life's grand and heroic adventures, overcoming the adversities strewn in their path. Black students moving onto formerly white campuses in greater numbers, writes black historian Vincent Harding, "must be so aware of their black fathers and the wealth of their spiritual and intellectual heritage that they will sharply illuminate the disadvantages inherent in an isolated, beleagured middle-class white world."

This desire among Afro-Americans to put history to the service of group uplift, long one of its functions in the hands of black writers, has made some historians uneasy. One prominent white historian, C. Vann Woodward, has voiced concern over what he interprets as efforts by blacks to turn their backs on history or to cast it in legendary or heroic molds. Another, Thomas A. Bailey, has expressed some fears about the insistence on "overvisibility," the "determination to stand American history on its head." Deplorable is "pressure group history of any kind . . . especially when significant white men are bumped out to make room for much less significant black men in the interests of social harmony." Granted such dangers to "true scholarship," much of this concern seems excessive and not a little condescending. It seems to be saying that we whites were only human when we omitted you from the pages of history or presented you in stereotype; you, however, should rise to the godly heights of dispassionate objectivity in your reflections on the past.

Addressing himself to the question of historical "objectivity" in a recent article in the *Saturday Review of Literature*, the black historian Benjamin Quarles has reminded us that historians no more than others can escape their past. In the case of the treatment of black people in the history texts this circumstance has meant that stereotypes inimical to them have been palmed off as "fact" when they have been made to appear at all. One facet of this problem, as Professor Quarles has suggested, has been that the black man has not had sufficient numbers of his own historians to "puff up his own kind" and to fight the war with the "stereotypers" on anything resembling even terms. And since the Afro-Americans' past has been different from that of other Americans, black folk can be expected to look at the American past through different eyes (as indeed they do), and to bring to it their own interpretations. The result will be the enlargement of the American past through a new vision. And this revision will simply be a part—an important part, to be sure—of that revisionism that seeks to bring the entire American past under new scrutiny. With the question of interpretation out of the way, I find myself in accord with some of these critics when they contend that no fabrication should be made—nor, indeed, is it necessary. Properly depicted and interpreted, the record of the Afro-American experience is one of which black people can be sufficiently proud.

Among the ironies and tragedies of the Afro-American past is that when, within the past decade, scholars began to pursue its study in earnest, they discovered that important beginnings had been made years earlier by such outstanding but little read black historians as W. E. B. DuBois and Carter Woodson. Over a busy life of writing and protesting, the versatile and talented DuBois found time to write about and promote the study of Afro-American history. The persistent Woodson was, if anything, even more committed to its promotion. He established the Association for the Study of Negro Life and History; he founded and for many years edited the *Journal of Negro History* (essential for the study of the Afro-American past); he originated and promoted the idea of Negro History Week. Had it not been for these Afro-American historians and their small group of followers, there would have been an almost total "blackout" of the Afro-American past. Or, to put it another way, there was a virtual "whitewash," for the American past as it issued from the pens and the podiums of white historians was devoid of the black man except for the footnote or the afterthought that he and the slave were one and the same. Taking their cue from DuBois and

Woodson, Afro-Americans are now demanding that the "blackout" be ended and *black* be given its rightful place *in* history.

If American blacks are awakening to the necessity of Afro-American history, so are many whites. To the white middle class the black revolution of our time, with its burning ghettos and its cries of black nationalism, is increasingly incomprehensible. And because no quick, dramatic solutions to the race problem have been forthcoming, white Americans have turned, like many others in periods of crisis, to history for assurance if not for answers. (*Black History: A Reappraisal*, a collection edited by Melvin Drimmer and published in 1968, is an example of this trend as well as a response to it.) It is indeed important that they go to history. It is important that they begin to familiarize themselves with a past that has been far from exclusively white. Whether or not they have known it, there has been a common journey on this continent in the past, and it will be a common journey in the future, or, many blacks have determined, there will be none. The race problem has always been more a white problem than a black one. By the same token, although the focus of Afro-American history must be on the black experience, on what blacks have said and done, that history must also include what whites have said about them and what they have done to them. For, as LeRoi Jones wrote in *Home: Social Essays*, "The paradox of the Negro experience in America is that it is a separate experience, but inseparable from the complete fabric of American life."

Might it be too much to contend that coming to grips with this "paradox" would force the overhauling of American history? Perhaps. But its study would certainly suggest several new perspectives for viewing the American past. Most important is a long-needed tragic dimension, which might cause us to alter our view of ourselves as a people by complementing, if not supplanting, the prevailing optimistic view of America and her destiny.*

There can be no escape from the reality of oppression in the black pilgrimage in America. Ample evidence of victimization and humiliation exists in the Afro-American past and present: in the long night of slavery, when the pattern of racism was set; in Reconstruction, when a golden opportunity to deal honestly and firmly with the problem of black freedom was lost; in the period following, when Jim Crow or the new slavery was fastened on the country; and in the present urban era of *de facto* segregation. Take, for example, the black ghetto.

The origins of the black metropolis go back to a time even before slavery was outlawed in the Northern states. Since the end of Reconstruction, however, the tempo of black migration to Southern cities, and out of the ancestral South to Northern centers, has continually accelerated. This mass movement of oppressed humanity has merely intensified all those problems that from the beginning stemmed from white supremacy and unequal opportunity: race wars, in which black city dwellers were the victims of white brutality; appalling housing, for which they paid more and received less; the most menial, lowest-income jobs, to which they have clung with a tenacity born of desperation; schools that have increasingly become ill-suited to the needs of the majority of Afro-American children; and policemen who make "very bad use of their power." In an article in *The Journal of American History*, Professor Gilbert Osofsky has rather neatly summed up the problem: "What has in our time been called the social pathology of the ghetto is evident throughout our history; the wounds

---

* For many of these thoughts on tragedy I am indebted to Vincent Harding's essay "The Uses of the Afro-American Past," reprinted in *Negro Digest*, February 1968, and Samuel DuBois Cook's "A Tragic Conception of Negro History," *Journal of Negro History*, October 1960.

of centuries have not healed because they have rarely been treated. By all the standard measurements of human troubles in the city, the ghetto has been with us—it has tragically endured." The extent of the bitterness now spilling out of the dark ghetto simply cannot be grasped without some appreciation of the tragic sameness of conditions over the generations.

If we are to comprehend more profoundly the meaning of the Afro-American past, however, we must consider another aspect of that tragedy. DuBois once said that there was something strange and holy about the ghetto's Saturday night. This great and bold man, Lerone Bennett has pointed out, was talking "not about blacks but about life: good and bad, preachers and prostitutes, gin and champagne, tragedy and triumph, having and not having, giving and taking, losing and winning—Life." In a recent interview in *Harper's,* the Afro-American novelist Ralph Ellison stated that "literature teaches us that mankind has always defined itself *against* the negatives thrown it by both society and the universe. It is human will, human hope, and human effort which make the difference. Let's not forget the great tragedies not only treat of negative matters of violence, brutality, defeats, but they treat them within a context of man's will to act, to change reality, and to snatch triumph from the teeth of destruction." Men have always discovered the need to affirm themselves, even—indeed, especially —in the face of suffering, humiliation, and degradation.

The case of slavery and the Afro-American reaction to it are instructive. The view has become widespread— among historians since the publication of Stanley Elkins's book, *Slavery*—that slavery in the United States was such a closed, authoritarian system that it robbed the slaves of virtually the last iota of humanity. That it was replete with suffering, pain, and sorrow is undeniable, but that it so "dehumanized" the slave as to reduce him to the "good

humor of everlasting childhood" is questionable. For if
one directs his attention to Afro-American folksongs and
folktales, utilizing the growing body of work in anthro-
pology, ethnomusicology, and folklore, he discovers that
despite the dependency complex that the "peculiar institution" engendered in many, the slaves were not reduced to
the level of "Sambo."* What Afro-American folklore reveals is that, in the words of the folklorist B. A. Botkin
(in *Lay My Burden Down: A Folk History of Slavery*):
". . . in spite of all attempts to crush it, the slave had a
will of his own, which was actively, as well as passively,
opposed to the master's. And it is this stubborn and rebel-
lious will—tragic, heroic, defeated, or triumphant—that,
more than all else, haunts us, as it haunted the master. . . ."
This is well illustrated in that Afro-American folk creation,
Brer Rabbit. "The American Negro slave," Arna Bontemps
has written, "adopting Brer Rabbit as hero, represented him
as the most frightened and helpless of creatures. No hero-
animals in Africa or elsewhere were so completely lacking
in strength. But the slaves took pains to give Brer Rabbit
other significant qualities. He became in their stories by
turn a practical joker, a braggart, a wit, a glutton, a lady's
man, and a trickster. But his essential characteristic was
his ability to get the better of bigger and stronger animals.
To the slave in his condition the theme of weakness overcoming strength through cunning proved endlessly fasci-
nating." Without the existence of this body of lore suggested
by Brer Rabbit, which was the product of the creative
energies and native wit of black folk, the slaves would
not have survived their ordeal with their essential humanity
intact. For these and similar reasons I can only agree with

* A most suggestive essay, to which I am much indebted for insights
into the use of Afro-American folklore, is Sterling Stuckey, "Through
the Prism of Folklore: The Black Ethos in Slavery," *The Massachusetts
Review*, Summer 1968.

Staughton Lynd's belief (expressed in *Class Conflict, Slavery and the United States Constitution*) that slavery is "one of the two or three distinctive themes of the American experience."

Ample evidence of the same tragic dimension is to be found in the present. Afro-American psychiatrists William H. Grier and Price M. Cobbs, in their recent book, *Black Rage*, relate the story of the black mother, prematurely old and on welfare, who in the midst of telling of her problems and sufferings could with genuine humor acknowledge and laugh at her own shortcomings. "At the end of the hour she dried her eyes, rearranged her wig, and strode out. As she moved, a particular style came through. She was depressed, upset, angry, and had her share of problems. She moved slowly, but her head was high. She disappeared down the hall. One knew that in the agony of her life was the beauty and torment of the black experience in this country." Replete with this kind of unobtrusive heroism and moral courage, the Afro-American past and present clearly demonstrate the capacity and determination of the race to endure and to survive with self-respect. It is a record of which no people need be ashamed.

Even though black folk have never believed in the idea of progress to the same extent that whites have, they have nonetheless maintained an optimistic faith that has astounded many. That faith has rested on a primitive Christianity and the resilience of their own indomitable souls. But as the events of recent years clearly demonstrate, Afro-Americans, especially the young, will no longer endure with quiet dignity and repressed rage the lowly position assigned to them by a society in which a significant number of people continue to believe in white supremacy. Black writer Lerone Bennett has warned: ". . . we must understand, and quickly, that the faith of the grandmother or grandfather is not the faith of the granddaughter or grandson. Too many people are dead in the coliseum, too many lies have been told for men to believe in the old way if, indeed, they find it possible to believe at all. The wheel of faith is turning in the ghetto and the fire is growing cold. The black man cannot and will not stand forever in the wings offering the gifts of pain and passion and renewal."

A study of the Afro-American past, with its tragedy and its irony, would do much to alter our romantic notion that the United States has been destined from its inception to escape the tragedies and ambiguities that have been the fate of other nations. The Afro-American story tells us that this country has been given no such exemption. It points up that Americans have developed no special immunity to the greed, folly, and cruelty that have characterized the behavior of other people. Myths aside, as Afro-American historian John Hope Franklin has written: ". . . this land was peopled, from the beginning, with ordinary human beings—very fallible human beings. They made mistakes, many mistakes. And they were wrongheaded in many ways." A study of the Afro-American past would help demythologize the American past by stripping from it much of the conceit and deception which surround it.

It may be, for example, that we might then entertain the idea that the roots of American culture lie in Africa as well as Europe. It should not be forgotten that black people have been in the Americas from the beginnings of the transatlantic crossing. In many places they were densely concentrated, and thus, to an extent formerly thought impossible, were able to cling to African values. Over time, of course, these values were modified by the New World experience. Modified, they survived: in dance, in music, in folklore, in speech, in religion. Most of all they survived, in Lerone Bennett's words, in that "certain dark joy—a zest for life, a creative capacity for meeting adversity and transcending it—that is beautiful and meaningful." The African and his New World descendants have not tended to view, as have white Christians, good and evil, body and soul, the here and the hereafter, as two separate coins, but as two sides of the same coin.

Living side by side as the two races have in the South, it would be absurd to assume (as so many people have) that the white influenced the black but in turn remained uninfluenced by him. Lillian Smith intimates otherwise: "It was natural that the white man was drawn to [the black man]. Laughter, song, rhythm, spontaneity were like a campfire in a dark tangled forest full of sins and boredom and fears. So bright, so near. . . ." And with reference to the country as a whole, Lerone Bennett has written: "Had there been no Negroes here, *had there been no darkness at all, this would be a pale and a lonely land.* / No Negroes? / What would we sing? / No darkness? / What would we dance? / No blackness? / What would we fear? How would we experience the boundaries and the whiteness of our lives?" How, indeed? The Afro-American has had an enduring effect upon the national character. "In our image of the Negro breathes the past we deny," James Baldwin has written, "not dead but living yet and powerful, the best in our jungle of statistics."

In an important recent book, *White Over Black*, Professor Winthrop Jordan addresses himself to the relationship of race and national identity in the early days of the Republic. The Revolutionary generation was faced with an identity crisis. Who were these newly independent people? Having severed the political link, they were no longer Englishmen. But most of them were of English descent, English was the national tongue, and English political and social institutions were regnant. They were, perhaps, some kind of modified Englishmen. In the midst of all this psychological and cultural confusion there was, however, that

that we carry on our backs in our foreign relations in the 1960s is the problem of racial discrimination at home. There is just no question about it." Indeed, how can we expect to understand, much less identify with, the wretched of Vietnam or South Africa when we are paralyzed with fear of the black man in our midst? Or they us? Is it not possible that the Afro-American, that "old-newcomer," could help us bridge the chasm? Precisely because his has been an experience of pain and sorrow, his may well be the authentic voice of liberation. The late Richard Wright once aptly remarked in *White Man, Listen!*: "Is it not clear to you that the American Negro is the only group in our nation that consistently and passionately raises the question of freedom? This is a service to America and to the world. More than this: The voice of the American Negro is rapidly becoming the most representative voice of America and of oppressed people anywhere in the world today." If we live in a world of increasing limitations, one can hope that this world is still one of opportunities.

There has been a common journey of black and white on this continent. The national character has been molded by the interaction of the two groups. But, because of greed and guilt, the black presence has been systematically omitted from our historic frame of reference. This has been the tragedy of tragedies: that we have not only oppressed the black man, but we have failed to recognize in his experience a means of liberating all of us. We must familiarize ourselves—and quickly—with the Afro-American experience past and present: with its sorrow, its joy, its suffering, its endurance; with its tragedy. Might we not then begin to question our belief in our moral omnipotence? And though the past would not seem to hold out much hope of it, might we not be then more willing to expose ourselves to suffering and humiliation? The experience need not be all that bitter. After all, as Ralph Ellison has said about the Afro-American odyssey: ". . . theirs has been one of the great human experiences and one of the great triumphs of the human spirit in modern times. In fact, in the history of the world."

2. JOSEPH LOGSDON

Diary of a Slave: Recollection and Prophecy

For more than half of this nation's history, black Americans were held in bondage, and the history of the Negro in the United States was shaped by the environment of the plantation South and the experience of slavery.

A Dutch privateer brought the first Africans to Virginia in 1619, a year before the Pilgrims landed at Plymouth. Although these blacks may at first have been treated much like other indentured servants, racial prejudice was almost immediately evident and a structure of discriminatory legislation quickly arose. By the 1660s, slavery—a status unknown to white colonists—had gained statutory recognition throughout the colonies. At the same time, pressure from the Restoration government in London caused the importation of African slaves to increase rapidly. By the time of the American Revolution, Africans made up the largest non-English element in the colonial population; and although there were a few free, or, more properly, quasi-free blacks, the great mass of Colonial blacks were slaves.

The first national census following the adoption of the Constitution disclosed that nine-tenths of the nation's 750,000 blacks were concentrated in the south Atlantic states. The ratio of slaves to free blacks shifted drastically as one moved north, revealing a rapid decline of slavery in the middle states and New England. While less than one-twentieth of all Southern blacks were free men, only one-fourth of New England Negroes remained slaves. Liberal sentiments and economic considerations combined to bring about the gradual abolition of slavery in the North during the two decades after the Revolution, but fear of the social consequences of a large free black population and the growing cotton cultivation implanted slavery more firmly than ever in Southern soil. After 1790 the slave population increased rapidly, rising to roughly two million by 1830 and to almost twice that number by 1860.

On the eve of the Civil War, most blacks, including more than half of those who were legally free, lived in Southern states. The lot of the free blacks was generally a miserable one, barely preferable to slavery. Economic opportunities were narrowly limited, and even in the North the blacks were discriminated against and denied their rights as members of the community. The conditions of life under slavery varied greatly throughout the region. Urban slaves, who were often artisans and sometimes given wide latitude, felt the burdens of their status less than those forced to work on farms and plantations. There, the attitudes of the master, the size of the operation, and the slave's position within the hierarchy of the plantation determined the treatment accorded the individual slave. Historians interested in the social structure of the white South have pointed out that nearly half of the slaveholders held fewer than five slaves, and that on such farms slaves and masters often toiled together in the fields. However, it must be remembered that more than two-thirds of those held in bondage served on plantations with more than ten slaves, and by all accounts such plantations, run by overseers who exercised nearly unlimited authority, witnessed the greatest incidence of cruelty and brutality.

The effect of this environment upon the personality development of the enslaved race has evoked continuing historical argument. One group of historians has emphasized the rebelliousness of the slaves and reasserted a faith in the common desire of all men to be free. A second group has taken the contrasting view that there were, in fact, few actual slave revolts, and that this fact is to be explained by the effect of "absolute power" of the master class on the slave personality. In the following essay, Professor Joseph Logsdon of Lehigh University subjects these alternative hypotheses to intensive examination in an area of the Deep South where slavery was notoriously oppressive. Making use of Solomon Northup's journal, Twelve Years a Slave, *Professor Logsdon shows that the slaves along Louisiana's Bayou Boeuf constantly plotted ways to escape their station, although the odds facing them were nearly insurmountable. Then, to test the response of these same slaves to the opportunity for freedom, Professor Logsdon carefully examines the results of the brief Union Army foray into the area in 1863 during the drive to capture Port Hudson and control of the lower Mississippi. The results of this investigation are impressive and cannot be ignored by historians and social scientists interested in the psychological effect of slavery; for Logsdon shows that the roles developed as defense mechanisms within the system were easily shed when the opportunity to break out of the system became available.*

In recent years, the historical debate over American slavery, after seeming resolution, has been renewed. The old racist canards, of course, have largely been dismissed, and few persons would any longer defend the institution on moral grounds. Nevertheless, some of the *old* controversies have been reopened and continued. The profitability of slavery or its role in causing the Civil War can still evoke spirited discussion. Now, however, new concerns and new methods of investigation dominate the literature. In agreement over the immorality of slavery and the equality of races, historians are taking another look at the

institution and are asking new questions about the slaveholder and the slave. Of the slaveholder: Were the planters
aggressive, commercial capitalists, or were they a feudal
leadership class with a paternalistic sense of communal
responsibility? Of the slave: Was he a freedom-loving,
resentful captive, or was he molded into a submissive,
docile victim? And of the system as a whole: Why were
there so few major slave revolts in the United States?

Admirable and impressive scholarship has gone into this
debate. Bilingual scholars have drawn provocative com-
parisons between North and South American slave systems.
The modern methods and the data of social psychology
have been called upon for analysis and speculation. The
transformed personalities of inmates in Nazi concentration
camps and American total prison systems have been probed
to explain the impact of slavery upon its victims. Discussion of these new questions has not always been dispassionate. Still, there has been less angry accusation than in
the past. Textbook writers, nonetheless, continue to find
the chapters on slavery difficult to write today. The current debate is not drawn along sectional lines; there are,
in fact, no easy lines to draw. Neither general background
nor ideological persuasion places the debaters into neatly
opposing camps. Yet a vigorous debate continues. To resolve the controversy, both textbook writers and some
debaters have called for further investigation and, interest-
ingly, investigation carried out "by the more orthodox pro-
cedures of historical research."

Where should we begin? Perhaps it would be wise to
return to a concluding remark made by Kenneth Stampp
—the last historian to make a thorough investigation of
the available manuscripts that record the workings of
American slavery. He ended his book in 1956 with a
"simple and chastening truth for those who would try to
understand the meaning of bondage." He chose the words

of a former slave: " 'Tisn't he who has stood and looked
on that can tell you what slavery is,—'tis he who has
endured."

Many have had their say on slavery; "but in our times,"
as another author put it recently, "we have forgotten the
testimony of its victims." It is clear that few American
historians have ever perused the slave testimony which has
survived. Perhaps the most surprising fact about this literature is how much has been preserved. A recent scholar
found more than sixty slave narratives and suggested that
there were many more.

Justifiable caution has kept some historians from relying
on these accounts. Some were forged, and most were tran-
scribed by abolitionists for use in their propaganda campaigns. Still, few scholars have been willing to test the
reliability of these essential documents. Apart from the
Narrative of Frederick Douglass, few of these autobiographies are familiar to the American reading public—or, for
that matter, to professional historians. This oversight has
been a serious mistake. Any renewed investigation of
American slavery must begin with these neglected accounts.
They can provide us with insights to test current theories,
lead us into new areas of research, and, by lifting the cloak
of the slave's anonymity, convert chattels into identifiable
human beings.

The value of this approach can be explored by selecting
one of these neglected narratives and examining its por-
trayal of human bondage in America. A persuasive illustration would be the narrative of Solomon Northup, *Twelve
Years a Slave.* Although there are few works in American
literature, even in fiction, that compare with this astound-
ing tale, Solomon Northup's story has seldom been read
in modern times. Our failure to read it, however, has deprived us not only of an exciting story, but also of a fruitful
source of historical insights.

I

The man's story is extraordinary. Solomon Northup was a free man, the son of an emancipated New England slave. Until the spring of 1841, he lived a simple, uneventful life with his wife and three children in upstate New York. Then, suddenly, at the age of thirty-two he fell victim to a series of bizarre events that make his one of the most tragic autobiographies ever written. In late March 1841, Northup accepted an offer from two strangers in Saratoga, New York, to catch up with a traveling circus and play in its band. But when the chase ended, Northup had been drugged, beaten, and sold to a slavetrader in Washington, D.C. Robbed of his identity and given the name "Platt," he was subsequently shipped to New Orleans, where he was purchased by a planter in the Red River region of Louisiana. For the next twelve years, Northup lived as a chattel under several masters. He might well have continued in that status and died an anonymous slave, except for another set of equally bizarre circumstances which enabled him to regain his freedom and tell his story to the world.

This sensationalism, which made for an exciting story, might legitimately call the narrative's historical value into question. Nevertheless, despite the almost unbelievable aspects of Northup's story, the leading students of American slavery—whatever their persuasion—have recognized its plausibility and value. Perhaps the sensational events themselves help to explain the book's usefulness and reliability.

The tragic turn in Northup's life gave him a unique set of qualifications for observation and analysis. He entered slavery educated and surprisingly well-traveled for his time. He was curious and fully aware of his former freedom and dignity. Without that prior experience, it is doubtful whether he would have presented so detailed and accurate a description of slave life and plantation society. There are many other travel accounts of the Old South, but the visitors who wrote about slavery only observed it; they did not endure its hardships. Neither the veil of color nor the barriers of status obscured Northup's vision. He shared the experiences of Southern slaves both as an outside critic and as a fellow black chattel. No other commentator on American slavery has those credentials.

No other slave, moreover, has left such a detailed picture of slavery in the Gulf South—the dynamic locale of the "peculiar institution" during the three decades before the Civil War. Relatively few slaves ever managed to win their freedom from this region, either by manumission or by escape. Almost all the slave narrators, therefore, came from the border states or the Atlantic seaboard. Without the legal assistance due him as a kidnaped citizen of New York, Solomon Northup would surely have died—silent—along the banks of the Red River in Louisiana.

Northup's experience provides still other reasons for its usefulness. As a citizen of New York, he could tell his full story immediately without any fear of recapture. Unlike most other fugitives, for whom publicity was a danger, he did not have to abbreviate his account or postpone it until after the Civil War. Nor did he have to seek solace among abolitionists and look back on slavery through their perspective. He returned to his old home, a normal community in upper New York.

His return to Glens Falls on the evening of January 20, 1853, kept the local area buzzing for some time. The morning after the reunion with his family, a large reception was held for him in a neighboring town. During that reception, or shortly thereafter, a local lawyer named David Wilson arranged to help Northup publish his autobiography. Wilson was the region's leading literary figure. A former superintendent in the area's public schools, he had already written some poetry and local history. None of his writing was ideological or polemic. Moreover, although he was a minor politician, his writing was never partisan. The Democratic newspaper in his home town indicated his reputation in the community by gracefully accepting his election to the state legislature the previous fall: "Mr. Wilson is not only one of the most eloquent orators at the bar, but one of the purest and sweetest poets in northern New York. We are sorry he is a Whig."

This information is important, for, unlike most of the ghost writers of slave narratives, Wilson was not an abolitionist. This is not to suggest that abolitionist involvement negates the value of other slave narratives, but simply to dismiss it as an issue in evaluating Northup's recollection and judgment. Although the prose style of the book belongs to David Wilson, there is no reason to doubt his statement, in the original preface to the book, that he had dedicated himself to an accurate transcription of Northup's reminiscences.

In the last analysis, Solomon Northup's narrative deserves to be believed, not simply because he *seems* to be talking reasonably, nor merely because he adorns his tale with compelling and persuasive details. There are better grounds for judging its reliability. At every point where materials exist to check his account, it can be verified. His descriptions of the region of his enslavement are unquestionably accurate in their smallest detail.

Many of the particulars of his story were also verified in several court appearances. Before his book was published, he brought the Washington slave traders to trial. That trial was aborted by the refusal of the Washington, D.C., court to accept a Negro's testimony against a white man. But, before it ended, it confirmed much about Northup's tale. After the book had been published, he apprehended his Northern kidnapers on the Fourth of July, 1853, and brought them before a New York court. Once again Northup's oppressors were released on technicalities. But this time his own testimony (valid in New York) and that of others gave further proof of his assertions. Few contemporaries, at least, doubted the guilt of the kidnapers.

Justice never came to Solomon Northup, either in the South or in the North. For his stolen years he received only a pathetic recompense—$3,000 for selling the copyright of his memoirs. With that sum he purchased some property and tried to pick up his life where he had left it in 1841. What finally became of Solomon Northup can only be conjectured. He probably died in 1863. Perhaps his last years, though, are unimportant. His recollection of slavery was his tragic bequest to mankind. This was the judgment, at least, of the firm which republished his memoirs after the Civil War. Their conclusion is still valid today:

To take in or to understand the exact status of such a people in all its bearings, we can pursue no better course than to live among them, to become one of them, to fall from a condition of freedom to one of bondage, to feel the scourge, to bear the marks of the brands, and the outrage of manacles. . . . It can be taken for what it is worth—a personal narrative of personal sufferings and keenly felt and strongly resented wrongs; but in our opinion, the individual will be lost or merged in the general interest and the work will be regarded as a history of an institution which our political economy has now happily superseded, but which, however much its existence may be regretted, should be studied—indeed, must be studied—by everyone whose interest in our country incites him to obtain a correct knowledge of her past existence.

II

The first and perhaps most lasting impression gained from Northup's narrative is the cruelty of slavery. Beatings of himself and others are described in all their brutality. His first, at the hands of the slave traders in Washington, is hard to forget. He begins his recollection of it by recalling the first words of the trader, spoken shortly after he recovered in a slave pen from the effects of his drugging:

"Well, my boy, how do you feel now?" said Burch, as he entered through the open door. I replied that I was sick, and inquired the cause of my imprisonment. He answered that I was his slave—that he had bought me, and that he was about to send me to New Orleans. I asserted, aloud and boldly, that I was a free man—a resident of Saratoga, where I had a wife and children, who were also free, and that my name was Northup. I complained bitterly of the strange treatment I had received, and threatened, upon my liberation, to have satisfaction for the wrong. He denied that I was free, and with an emphatic oath declared that I came from Georgia. Again and again I asserted I was no man's slave, and insisted upon his taking off my chains at once. He endeavored to hush me, as if he feared my voice would be overheard. But I would not be silent, and denounced the authors of my imprisonment, whoever they might be, as unmitigated villains. Finding he could not quiet me, he flew into a towering passion. With blasphemous oaths he called me a black liar, a runaway from Georgia, and every other profane and vulgar epithet that the most indecent fancy could conceive.

During this time Radburn was standing silently by. His business was, to oversee this human, or rather inhuman stable, receiving slaves, feeding and whipping them, at the rate of two shillings a head per day. Turning to him, Burch ordered the paddle and cat-o'-ninetails to be brought in. He disappeared, and in a few moments returned with these instruments of tor-

ture. The paddle, as it is termed in slave-beating parlance, or
at least the one with which I first became acquainted, and of
which I now speak, was a piece of hardwood board, eighteen
or twenty inches long, moulded to the shape of an old-fashioned
pudding stick, or ordinary oar. The flattened portion, which was
about the size in circumference of two open hands, was bored
with a small auger in numerous places. The cat was a large
rope of many strands—the strands unraveled, and a knot tied
at the extremity of each.

As soon as these formidable whips appeared, I was seized
by both of them, and roughly divested of my clothing. My feet,
as has been stated, were fastened to the floor. Drawing me over
the bench, face downwards, Radburn placed his heavy foot
upon the fetters, between my wrists, holding them painfully to
the floor. With the paddle, Burch commenced beating me. Blow
after blow was inflicted upon my naked body. When his un-
relenting arm grew tired, he stopped and asked if I still insisted
I was a free man. I did insist upon it, and then the blows were
renewed, faster and more energetically, if possible, than before.
When again tired, he would repeat the same question, and receiving the same answer, continued his cruel labor. All this
time, the incarnate devil was uttering most fiendish oaths. At
length the paddle broke, leaving the useless handle in his hands.
Still I would not yield. All his brutal blows could not force
from my lips the foul lie that I was a slave. Casting madly on
the floor the handle of the broken paddle, he seized the rope.
This was far more painful than the other. I struggled with all
my power, but it was in vain. I prayed for mercy, but my
prayer was only answered with imprecations and with stripes.
I thought I must die beneath the lashes of the accursed brute.
Even now the flesh crawls upon my bones, as I recall the scene.
I was all on fire. My sufferings I can compare to nothing else
than the burning agonies of hell!

At last I became silent to his repeated questions. I would
make no reply. In fact, I was becoming almost unable to speak.
Still he plied the lash without stint upon my poor body, until
it seemed that the lacerated flesh was stripped from my bones
at every stroke. A man with a particle of mercy in his soul

would not have beaten even a dog so cruelly. At length Radburn said that it was useless to whip me any more—that I would be sore enough. Thereupon, Burch desisted, saying, with an admonitory shake of his fist in my face, and hissing the words through his firm-set teeth, that if ever I dared to utter again that I was entitled to my freedom, that I had been kidnapped, or anything whatever of the kind, the castigation I had just received was nothing in comparison with what would follow. He swore that he would either conquer or kill me. With these consolatory words, the fetters were taken from my wrists, my feet still remaining fastened to the ring; the shutter of the little barred window, which had been opened, was again closed, and going out, locking the great door behind them, I was left in darkness as before.

Northup learned fear from this beating by Burch; his accommodation to almost absolute power was swift. But this accommodation was not the result of a stunting of his personality; it was a rational decision, as he later explained. "I was too costly a chattel to be lost, and was well aware that I would be taken further on, into some by-place, over the Texas border, perhaps, and sold; that I would be disposed of as the thief disposes of his stolen horse, if my right to freedom was even whispered. So I resolved to lock the secret closely in my heart—never to utter one word or syllable as to who or what I was—trusting in Providence and my own shrewdness for deliverance."

Not all beating, however, was as purposeful as that administered by Burch to insure Northup's silence. Northup clearly indicates the results of such unlimited power on the slaveholder as well as the slave. Edwin Epps, the Louisiana planter who owned him for almost ten years, frequently in drunken rages beat his slaves for enjoyment. Even while sober, he showed sadistic tendencies. Northup showed insight in his evaluation of this man. It is clear that the slave understood the master better than the master knew the slave:

To speak truthfully of Edwin Epps would be to say—he is a man in whose heart the quality of kindness or of justice is not found. A rough, rude energy, united with an uncultivated mind and an avaricious spirit, are his prominent characteristics. He is known as a "nigger breaker," distinguished for his faculty of subduing the spirit of the slave, and priding himself upon his reputation in this respect, as a jockey boasts of his skill in managing a refractory horse. He looked upon a colored man, not as a human being, responsible for the small talent entrusted to him, but as a "chattel personal," as a mere live property, no better, except in value, than his mule or dog. When the evidence, clear and indisputable, was laid before him that I was a free man, and as much entitled to my liberty as he, . . . he only raved and swore, denouncing the law that tore me from him. . . . He thought of nothing but his loss, and cursed me for having been born free. He could have stood unmoved and seen the tongues of his poor slaves torn out by the roots—he could have seen them burned to ashes over a slow fire, or gnawed to death by dogs, if it only brought him profit. Such a hard, cruel, unjust man is Edwin Epps.

Northup had no doubt that slavery created fiendish and vicious men; he identified them by name. Perhaps one would expect such portraits. But he makes these frightening figures even more credible by making distinctions in the behavior of various planters. Considering the circumstances, he demonstrated extraordinary sensitivity in analyzing individual men. Of his first owner, William Ford (like Epps a Louisianian), Northup had rather pleasant memories. In speaking of him, he cautioned his readers against quick and easy judgment.

In many northern minds, perhaps, the idea of a man holding his brother man in servitude, and the traffic in human flesh, may seem altogether incompatible with their conceptions of a

moral or religious life. From descriptions of such men as Burch
and Freeman, and others hereinafter mentioned, they are led
to despise and execrate the whole class of slaveholders and
indiscriminately. But I was some time his slave, and had an
opportunity of learning well his character and disposition, and
it is but simple justice to him when I say, in my opinion, there
never was a more kind, noble, candid, Christian man than
William Ford. The influences and associations that had always
surrounded him, blinded him to the inherent wrong at the
bottom of the system of slavery. He never doubted the moral
right of one man holding another in subjection. Looking through
the same medium with his fathers before him, he saw things
in the same light. Brought up under other circumstances and
other influences, his notions would undoubtedly have been different. Nevertheless he was a model master, walking uprightly,
according to the light of his understanding, and fortunate was
the slave who came to his possession. Were all men such as he,
Slavery would be deprived of more than half its bitterness.

The bitterness, Northup explained, was not just the result
of physical brutality. The emotional impact was even more
severe. The heartbreaks caused by the separation of families
and friends, together with the daily humiliations of bondage,
are personalized in his account. He describes the emotions
of men and women whom he came to know intimately. For
some the impact upon individual personality was profound;
several close friends crumbled psychologically before his
eyes. Others he found already brutalized for reasons he
never discovered.

Yet he and many others survived any total breakdown
of their personalities. There was relief, he discovered, from
the physical and emotional punishment. Slaves learned to
outwit the planters; they established norms and standards
among themselves; and they found certain amenities that
made even human bondage endurable. He vividly portrays,
for example, the balm of holiday celebrations. Although a
cultural outsider, he came to appreciate the beauty and

joys of the slave folk arts. "The Christmas dance!" he
exclaimed. "Oh, ye pleasure-seeking sons and daughters of
idleness, who move with measured step, listless and snail-
like, through the slow winding cotillon, if ye wish to look
upon celerity, if not the 'poetry of motion'—upon genuine
happiness, rampant and unrestrained—go down to Louisiana and see the slaves dancing in the starlight of a Christmas night."

The resilience of the human spirit, Northup maintained,
ran high among the slaves. Even among those who, at first,
seemed crushed by bondage, he found hope. Sometimes the
assertion of humanity and a sense of injustice surprised
Northup. Courageous acts of resistance and violence came
from individuals he considered altogether docile and retir-
ing. "It is a mistaken opinion that prevails in some circles,"
he declared, "that the slave does not understand the term—
does not comprehend the idea of freedom. Even on Bayou
Bouef, where I conceive slavery exists in its most abject
and cruel form—where it exhibits features altogether unknown in more northern States—the most ignorant of them
generally know full well its meaning. They understand the
privileges and exemptions that belong to it—that it would
bestow upon them the fruits of their own labors, and that
it would secure to them the enjoyment of domestic happiness."

Although Northup portrayed fine shadings of character
among both the slaves and the slaveholders, he never lost
sight of the institution as a whole. Here his judgment and
condemnation never wavered:

There may be humane masters, as there certainly are inhuman
ones—there may be slaves well-clothed, well-fed, and happy as
there are surely those half-clad, half-starved and miserable;
nevertheless, the institution that tolerates such wrong and in-
humanity as I have witnessed, is a cruel, unjust and barbarous
one. Men may write fictions portraying lowly life as it is, or

as it is not—may expatiate with owlish gravity upon the bliss
of ignorance—discourse flippantly from arm chairs of the pleas-
ures of slave life; but let them toil with him on husks; let them
behold him scourged, hunted, trampled on, and they will come
back with another story in their mouths. Let them know the
heart of the poor slave—learn his secret thoughts—thoughts he
dare not utter in the hearing of the white man; let them sit by
him in the silent watches of the night—converse with him in
trustful confidence, of "life, liberty, and the pursuit of happiness," and they will find that ninety-nine out of every hundred
are intelligent enough to understand their situation, and to
cherish in their bosoms the love of freedom, as passionately
as themselves.

In recent times, this sort of judgment about slavery has
come under attack. If the slave had such a sense of injustice, if he retained any notion of his own worth and dignity
—why, then, were there so few slave revolts? In answer-
ing this self-imposed question, historians seldom suggest
any longer that the infrequency of massive resistance im-
plied satisfaction or innate deficiencies of knowledge and
character. Rather, it is suggested that the American slave
system, the worst in the world, completely crushed the
slave's will to resist and transformed him into a submissive
and childlike sambo.

For this provocative hypothesis—one which has stirred
historical inquiry as few others have in recent times—there
is little proof in Northup's recollection of twelve years in
bondage. "Such an idea as insurrection," he insisted, "is not
new among the enslaved population of Bayou Boeuf." He
discovered from his fellow chattels that a careful conspiracy
had been put into operation several years before he arrived
in the Red River region. "It has become a subject of general and unfailing interest in every slave-hut on the bayou,
and will go down to succeeding generations as their chief
tradition." Their plan, as he heard it, was to set out for

Mexico. But before they could begin, their rallying point was discovered and the leader of the revolt, in anticipation of failure, warned the planters that the slaves intended to massacre the whites. Terror filled the whole countryside; both the conspirators and the innocent were taken to the scaffold. The indiscriminate slaughter did not stop until the planters themselves called in federal troops to pacify the area. The original leader and betrayer escaped punishment; he was, in fact, rewarded. The state legislature freed him by compensating his owner and gave him $500 to leave the area. He decided to stay in the area, but "his name," Northup insisted, "is despised and execrated by his race throughout the parishes of Rapides and Avoylles."

Even this betrayal and subsequent repression did not halt the hatching of insurrectionary schemes. Reason, and not docility, however, kept them from being put into operation. "More than once," Northup recalled, "I have joined in serious consultation, when the subject was discussed, and there have been times when a word from me would have placed hundreds of my fellow-bondsmen in an attitude of defiance. Without arms or ammunition, or even with them I saw such a step would result in certain defeat, disaster and death, and always raised my voice against it."

This was the recollection of a slave. It can be accepted or rejected. Although no one until recently has bothered to test its authenticity, historians have not been unaware of Northup's account. Some have used it and accepted his conclusions; others have simply dismissed it or not taken it very seriously. Although his facts are accurate, there is still sufficient ground to question and debate his observations and conclusions.

Northup seemingly anticipated these doubts in his own day. For ultimate vindication of his judgments, he turned to prophecy. He felt certain that future events would bear him out. "In my opinion," he began, "and I have had the opportunity to know something of the feeling of which I speak—there are not fifty slaves on the shores of Bayou Boeuf, but would hail with unmeasured delight the approach of an invading army. They are deceived who flatter themselves that the ignorant and debased slave has no conception of the magnitude of his wrongs. They are deceived who imagine that he arises from his knees, with back lacerated and bleeding, cherishing only a spirit of meekness and forgiveness. A day may come—it *will* come, if his prayer is heard—a terrible day of vengeance, when the master in his turn will cry in vain for mercy."

III

This prophecy by Northup can direct the historian to a possible breakthrough in the contemporary debate over slavery. The practice of examining American history within two segments sharply divided by the Civil War must come to an end. Particularly in analyzing slavery, historians must discard this old periodization. We must recognize that the dynamics of the institution continued through the bloody war and into our own time. The years of emancipation can be as valuable a source of investigation as the years of legalized slavery. The techniques of psychology can still be used; the insights from comparative slave systems may prove even more meaningful. But first we must open the Civil War curtain and watch the old characters—the slave, the slaveholder, and the antislavery critics—perform in this second act of the great American drama. The role of the black agricultural laborer did not end after the war broke out; it was merely extended through the Reconstruction era into modern times.

Northup as a character in the first act anticipated the unfolding of the plot in the second, even though he did not live to see it. The curtain rose along the Bayou Boeuf in the spring of 1863 about the time he died. That year a Union army, under the command of General Nathaniel Banks, marched up from the year-old Yankee base at New Orleans. The maneuver was designed to capture Port Hudson. Along with the Vicksburg campaign, this movement formed part of the overall strategy for opening the full length of the Mississippi River.

The troops marched through the country Northup knew so well. They took a railroad west to the sugar country, where his owners had frequently rented him during the cutting season. Marching northward along the Bayou Teche, the major waterway through this rich plantation country, the troops reached Opelousas, the old capital of the state. From there they set out for Alexandria along the banks of the Bayou Boeuf. The invading army had come, almost as if to test Northup's angry prophecy.

The scene in the plantation country fascinated the Yankee soldiers; many of them recorded their impressions. A soldier from the 114th New York Infantry Regiment recalled the reception:

The most noticeable feature of the Teche campaign was the great number of slaves, and the amusing manifestations of welcome they gave to their Yankee liberators. At every plantation, the road would be lined, and the fences covered, with black faces—men, women and children, courtesying and bowing, singing and dancing—all attempting to express their joy at once. . . . Most of them would have their bundles all ready to leave their homes, and fall in with the troops marching along. It required the most strenuous exertions to keep the army from being clogged with thousands of negroes.

The scene was the same along the Bayou Boeuf. Some slaves had been taken off by the hastily retreating Confederates, but the overwhelming number who remained behind became immediately defiant. Some even armed them-

selves and participated in a number of clashes. Many others
provided the Union army with vital intelligence about Confederate troop movements and assisted in foraging expedi-
tions. With apparent relish they helped Banks loot the
countryside of cotton and sugar, mountains of which were
piled high at docks for shipment to New Orleans.

Several of the soldiers had read Northup's account and
were well aware of the irony of this moment. Some searched
out those who knew Northup and spoke with them. One
recalled his visit with the original villain: "We passed the
Epps plantation, famous as being the home of Solomon
Northup, whose book made such a sensation in anti-slavery
circles some years ago. Old Epps yet lives, and told us that
a greater part of the book was truth and that many old
negroes remembered Northup."

The slaves definitely had remembered Northup, even
more of them, it seems, than Epps suspected. Another
reader of Northup's narrative went among the slaves to
speak with them about their former comrade: "Plenty of
negroes are found about here," he wrote, "who say that
they knew Platt well and have danced to the music of his
fiddle often. Some who remember when he was taken out
of the lot by the 'Northern gemman' . . . a scene which
made a lasting impression on the minds of the poor darkies
who saw the affair. The negroes are now free according to
the proclamation of Abe Lincoln. . . . Their freedom here
is conditioned with the stay of the troops in this portion
of the country."

The slaves apparently understood their status better than
the Union soldiers. What may well be the greatest single
exodus of servile people in modern times followed the withdrawal of Yankee forces from the area. Thousands had
already left with the produce-laden steamers for New Orleans, but thousands more marched out by foot, covering

an incredible 110 miles in five days, 36 by forced march under Confederate pursuit in the last twenty-four hours. A soldier described the beginning of the withdrawal:

The entire country was deprived of its laboring population. Every hour that they advanced added to the throng of negroes they had collected. Every plantation furnished its quota to the black multitude. Consternation preceded the movement of the soldiers, and the planters devised every means to conceal their slaves. . . . The blacks usually entered into the arrangement with much eagerness and delight, while the planters looked on perfectly thunderstruck at the infidelity of their servants.

This soldier's observation highlighted one of the most revealing episodes of this campaign: The planters were shocked by the behavior of the slaves. Field hands left *en masse*, and the behavior of the house servants was hardly different. The soldiers guffawed at the sight of white plantation belles in tugs-of-war with their favorite servants, or at the spectacle of mulatto servants streaming from windows of their attic prisons while their owners stood at the road smiling innocently at the passing caravan.

Just how surprised the planters were is revealed in these excerpts from the letters of a Bayou Boeuf planter, written immediately after the exodus:

The arrival of the advance of the Yankees alone turned the negroes crazy. They became utterly demoralized at once and everything like subordination and restraint was at an end. All business was suspended and those that did not go on with the army remained at home to do much worse. . . . I assure you for the space of a week they had a perfect jubilee. . . . Your boy Wallace and two others . . . forcibly put a Confederate soldier in the stocks at your place on Saturday night a week ago. They abused him too, very much. . . . The *drivers* everywhere have proved the worst negroes.

Several days later, when the slave stragglers and those taken off by the planters were returned, their attitudes were also reported by this same planter, first hand:

Things are just now beginning to work right—the negroes hated awfully to go to work again. Several have been shot and probably more will have to be. Chambers'—down here—have been acting very bad—and the overseer and five or six others ran off since Friday last. On Sunday the most of those left were whipped and matters are getting on better now. All the furniture at Elmfield was taken out of the house and taken to the negroes' cabins—and yesterday morning when I got there Y[ounger] was having it brought back. Old Frank and a number of others started too late—our cavalry turned them back—and now Frank says he never had any idea of going with them. The recent trying scenes through which we have passed have convinced me that *no dependence is to be placed on the negro* —and that they are the greatest hypocrites and liars that God ever made.

The uprising and outpouring of slaves from the Bayou Boeuf area was a monumental event in the Civil War. Despite the fact that General Banks considered this exodus "the gauge of our success in the campaign," recent historians have virtually ignored it. The soldiers, however, were impressed. One of them wrote a graphic description of the line of march as it passed him by:

In the history of the war, it is probable that another such sight was never witnessed. There can be no doubt that this was the greatest multitude of contrabands ever collected. It has been correctly stated that there were in this one procession, of upwards of four hundred carts and vehicles [actually there were almost a thousand], over eight thousand blacks. The regiment waited for hours, and still the apparently interminable line kept pouring by. [Most estimated it at nine miles long.] Every few minutes the boys would burst forth into shouts of merriment.

. . . Here came a mammoth plantation cart, filled with rough furniture, and screaming children, nearly nude, drawn by a pair of oxen. There came a young man leading a cow, upon whose horns and back was attached a rattling museum of frying pans, pails, grid-irons, old clothes and hoes. Next appeared a creaking wagon, in which was an old grey-headed couple, demurely sitting on a broken stove. Then came trudging along a bevy of bare-footed women with infants, papoose-like, on their backs. Presently a very ancient and ragged looking mule, with two or three women and children astride its back. Again would appear more plantation carts, covered with awnings of blankets, cowhides or boards. Then the attention would be attracted to an old man limping along with a cane, and carrying a half naked child astride his neck. Or the eye would fall upon a young wench, walking stiff and erect, with an enormous bundle upon her head. Occasionally an old vehicle would break down in the road, and scatter in the mud the most wonderful collection of furniture, utensils, clothing, and traps generally, that the mind can conceive of. Now and then some quaint establishment would have a runaway, tearing through the black ranks, upsetting everything in its mad career. Such incidents would call forth a variety of ejaculations from the frightened pedestrians.

They were mostly clothed in coarse grey cotton suits. A few, though, were decked off with the most expensive finery, which they had stolen from their masters or mistresses. All the women wore gaudy colored bandanas wrapped over their wooly pates, and the men generally had broad brimmed hats, much the worse for wear. The remarks made as they passed along were equally amusing. "O, bress de Lor'! I'se gwine to de promised land!" "I rekin as how ole mas'r has done lost two thousand dollar in dis chile, shoo. Yah! Yah!" "Dese Yankees are arful smart peple, dey are; dey make ole secesh folks jist tremble in der boots!" "I wonder if missus will miss dis yer bonnet?" "Please, Mr. Soger, whar we gwine at? When we cross over Jerdin?" The bare mention of the word *freedom*, to these poor people would throw them into perfect extacies [*sic*] and they would dance and shout in the most extravagant manner.

Freedom was the slaves' goal, not freedom from work, as many Northerners and Southerners would interpret it, but freedom probably as Northup had described it many years before—freedom "to dwell where the black man may work for himself—live in his own cabin—till his own soil. . . ." That dream never came true. The slaves were deceived.

The Yankee "liberators" thrust them back to the soil, to white man's soil as free laborers—free laborers who would again be locked on the land, this time by debt and deprivation. Even at the outset of this campaign, the army leaders were reluctant liberators. They did not come to free men; they planned to capture a fort and loot the countryside. Liberation was an afterthought.

The ambivalence of the army was clearly exposed when, in one area, the slaves rose up and armed themselves to free their fellows. This disciplined, mounted force under a Captain Pierre was routed by a spontaneous coalition of Union soldiers and local whites. Ten of the slaves' leaders were taken off and hanged from a bridge, and allowed to dangle for others to see.

The army did not come to Louisiana to liberate, and the slaves never found freedom. When the curtain closed on the second act of the American drama, the relative positions of the main characters—the slave, the slaveholders, and the antislavery critics—had not changed very much.

IV

The curtain for the third act has probably gone up already, in our own time. We are now the actors. Each must select his own role. Today not all the characters can be found along the banks of the Bayou Boeuf. The scenes are new. Ever since the 1930s, mechanization and agricultural diversification have sent descendants of the slaves to

Watts, Chicago, and Detroit. In these settings, the recent anger and bitterness of the oppressed once again shocks the oppressor. Few have bothered to read the narratives of twentieth-century blacks. But now, for many, the present once again throws surprising light upon the past.

Will the third act of the American drama turn it into a terrible tragedy? The answer will probably depend on whether the actors can, somehow, gain perspective on one another's historical roles, particularly the role of the oppressed. To appreciate the role of the black man in America, we will have to turn to his testimony of the past. That testimony may be of different kinds: sometimes the impassioned personal narrative; sometimes the decision to flee on the heels of the Union army; and, yes, sometimes armed rebellion in the rural countryside or the urban ghetto. But if we are ever to act with understanding, we must pay attention to him "who has endured." Looking over the diary of an ante-bellum slave may be a good place to start. That is, after all, where the drama began.

3. JAMES M. MCPHERSON

The Civil War and Reconstruction: A Revolution of Racial Equality?

The Civil War ended slavery, but political and social equality for black Americans remained a "deferred commitment." During the war, the Lincoln administration moved haltingly, prodded by Northern blacks and abolitionists, to attack slavery and break down discriminatory legislation in the North.

The year 1862 was, for the American Negro, what 1789 had been for the French peasant. In rapid succession, Congress abolished slavery in the District of Columbia and the territories, and declared the slaves of all those persons involved in open rebellion against the Union "forever free of their servitude." Lincoln, whose own attitudes evolved radically during these years, issued the preliminary Emancipation Proclamation in September, after the Union victory at Antietam, and on the first day of 1863 signed the final Emancipation Proclamation. All Negroes were not yet free, but the Union had made a commitment to freedom later honored in the Thirteenth Amendment.

As the administration moved to end slavery it also altered its recruitment policy and allowed the enlistment of black troops. By the end of the war, more than 200,000 Negroes served the Union. Poorly trained, subject to barbaric treatment if captured, and underpaid for most of the war, the "Sable Arm" of the Union war machine nonetheless distinguished itself for courage and devotion to the cause of freedom.

After the war and Lincoln's assassination, when the Southern states, with the blessing of Andrew Johnson's administration, attempted to rejoin the Union while maintaining the servile condition of the Southern Negro, the Radical Republicans in Congress enacted a harsh but necessary program for the reconstruction of the Southern states, designed to ease the transition from slavery to freedom and protect the Negro's civil rights. Finally, through the Fourteenth and Fifteenth Amendments, the Radicals wrote the principles of equality in civil and political rights into the Constitution.

Blacks gave the Radical program solid support in the North and formed the only dependable element in the Republican coalition in the South. The black masses eagerly fulfilled their duties as citizens; and their leaders functioned, in general, honestly and capably in a wide variety of positions, from local sheriffs to members of Congress.

However, the Reconstruction process was, as one might have expected given the problems it faced, chaotic, and was soon abandoned. In the early 1870s the Radicals enacted several measures to enforce the Reconstruction Amendments and a general civil rights law to end discrimination, but the tide was running against Radicalism. Northern whites, tired of "the eternal nigger," withdrew their support from the Republicans. The Democratic party, which cast itself in the role of defender of the white South during these years, swept the Congressional elections of 1874 and set out to reverse the work of the Radicals. Three years later, a Republican President, Rutherford B. Hayes, unable to enforce the Reconstruction Amendments and the civil rights legislation, withdrew the last federal troops from the South. The attempt to make real the dream of equality in the United States had tragically failed.

Historians have given a number of reasons for the "abandonment of the Negro during Reconstruction." The

Radicals' opponents attacked the corruption of the Re-construction governments, ascribing it to Negro participa-tion, and called for the return to power of the South's "natural leaders." The first generation of professional his-torians of Reconstruction adopted this view and empha-sized corruption, inefficiency, and the Radicals' ignorance of the "teaching of modern science" on the radical infe-riority of blacks as the main causes of the decline of the Radicals' influence. More recent historians have emphasized economic arguments: Depressed business conditions in the 1870s caused Northern businessmen to desire peace at any cost, class conflicts split the Radical coalition, and the economic ideology of the Republicans themselves inhibited effective federal action.

In this essay, Professor James McPherson of Princeton University outlines the view, held by most present-day scholars, that Reconstruction presented American society with the opportunity—a "golden opportunity," according to Professor Scruggs—to move toward the solution of the nation's race problem. That this was not done represents, for Professor McPherson, the failure of Reconstruction; a failure not only in terms of our contemporary situation, but also in relation to the best sympathies of the postwar generation. After carefully weighing the various elements which produced this failure, Professor McPherson con-cludes that the limited commitment of Northerners to racial equality was the crucial factor which gave each of the others meaning.

MORE than forty years ago Charles Beard, one of the country's leading historians, described the Civil War era as the Second American Revolution. Beard maintained that Northern victory transferred political and economic power from the old Southern planter aristocracy to the new

Northern industrial plutocracy and set in motion the ex-
plosive economic growth of the last third of the nineteenth
century. Whatever the validity of Beard's argument (it has
been challenged by several economic historians), there is
no doubt that in the field of race relations the Civil War
and Reconstruction did produce revolutionary changes. In
a period of less than ten years, four million slaves were
emancipated by the force of arms, enfranchised by the
national government, and granted equal civil and political
rights by the United States Constitution. But this was an
aborted revolution; the promise of racial equality was never
fully implemented even during Reconstruction; and after
1877, black Americans were gradually repressed into
second-class citizenship, from which they are emerging
slowly and painfully in our own time. This essay will try
to describe the potential revolution of racial equality a
century ago and to analyze the reasons for its failure.

Northern war aims evolved through three stages during
the Civil War. The earliest and most important war aim,
of course, was restoration of the Union. Until late in 1862
this meant the Union "as it was"—with slavery still in it.
The North did not go to war to abolish slavery, and it
took more than a year of discussion and agitation to bring
the government to a policy of emancipation. Despite his
own abhorrence of slavery, Abraham Lincoln was sensitive
to the pressures of proslavery conservatives in the North
and the need to keep the border slave states in the Union.
The election of 1860 had shown that most Northerners,
although opposed to the expansion of slavery into new
territories, were not in favor of abolishing it where it already existed. The Constitution protected slavery; and
Lincoln hoped that he could bring about restoration of
the Union constitutionally with a demonstration of federal
force and a short war, followed by political negotiations
and compromise.

But there were a good many people in the North who wanted to make emancipation a second war aim. These abolitionists (black and white), and Radical Republicans, believed that slavery had caused the war and that Union victory was impossible without elimination of this festering sore. The Radicals, joined by a growing number of moderates, argued with telling effect that emancipation was a military necessity. They pointed out that the 3½ million slaves in the Confederacy constituted more than one-third of its population, raised most of the food and fiber for the South, and did most of the digging, hauling, and construction work for the Confederate army. A blow against slavery would cripple the Southern war effort and attract thousands of freed blacks to the side of the North, where they could work and fight, not only for their own freedom, but for the Union as well.

The military necessity thesis was the most compelling argument for emancipation, but abolitionists also emphasized political and moral considerations. Politically, an antislavery policy would strengthen the Union's diplomatic efforts to keep Great Britain from helping the South, for English public opinion would not tolerate its government's intervention on the side of slavery against freedom. The Radicals also pointed out that even if the Union could be restored by negotiation and compromise, slavery would remain a source of future strife. There could be no internal peace in America, they argued, while four million people were in bondage. Moreover, the North professed to be fighting for the preservation of democratic government; the national anthem declared the Union to be the "land of the free and the home of the brave." But the Northern policy of fighting for the restoration of a slave-holding Union, said the abolitionists, made a mockery of this profession.

By 1862, mainly as a result of developments in the war

itself, these arguments began to gain converts. The Confederacy won most of the major battles in the first seventeen months of the war, and a serious danger of British intervention on the side of the South existed in 1862. War weariness and defeatism lowered Northern morale. Lincoln's conservative policy toward slavery alienated the Radical wing of his party. As these pressures built up Lincoln and the Republican Congress took timid and then decisive action against slavery in the second year of the war. Congress passed a series of antislavery and confiscation acts, and in September of 1862 the President issued a preliminary Emancipation Proclamation, stating that all the slaves in states still in rebellion on January 1, 1863, would be freed. The South was still in rebellion on that date, so Lincoln issued his final Emancipation Proclamation. Henceforth, the North officially fought for freedom as well as union.

Thus the second war aim was proclaimed, to be confirmed by Northern victory and the adoption of the Thirteenth Amendment in 1865. Well before the end of the war, however, Radicals began calling for a third war aim: civil equality for the freedmen. The antislavery ideals of abolitionists and Radical Republicans envisioned not only freedom for black people, but a positive guarantee of equal rights as well. Gradually, fitfully, haltingly, and with doubtful conviction, the North groped toward a commitment to equality as its third war aim; but never was equality so important an objective as Union and emancipation. Many Northerners who supported or accepted emancipation as a military necessity were notably unenthusiastic about this third war aim. It is necessary, not only for a comprehension of the Civil War and Reconstruction but also of the race problem in our own time, to understand the incomplete and halting efforts a century ago to implement equality and the reasons why they failed.

The first step toward equality was the enlistment of black men in the Union army. As Frederick Douglass put it: "Once let the black man get upon his person the brass letters, *U.S.*, let him get an eagle on his button, and a musket on his shoulder and bullets in his pocket, and there is no power on earth which can deny that he has earned the right to citizenship." Undertaken tentatively as an experiment late in 1862, the employment of Negro soldiers proved a success and was prosecuted on a full scale in the last two years of the war. In a sense, this result was a logical outgrowth of emancipation; for one of the purposes of freeing the slaves was to deprive the Confederacy of a vital manpower resource and utilize that resource for the Union, not only by getting black men to dig trenches and haul supplies for the Northern armies (the sort of work slaves did for the South), but by putting them into uniform to fight for Union and freedom.

Despite the initial skepticism of many Northerners, including President Lincoln, black men demonstrated impressive fighting qualities. In a series of battles all over the South in the last two years of war, Negro troopers proved their courage and determination. Thirty-eight black regiments fought in the Union armies that invaded Virginia in 1864, helping to deliver the hammer blows that finally drove Lee's forces to surrender. Negroes were the first soldiers to enter Charleston and Richmond when these important strongholds fell late in the war. By the time the war was over, about 180,000 black men, most of them former slaves, had fought for the Union army, and another 25,000 had served in the navy. More than 37,000 black soldiers lost their lives in the defense of union and freedom. Twenty-one Negroes won Congressional Medals of Honor for their courage on the field of battle. Black troops numbered nearly 10 per cent of the total Union forces and constituted an even higher percentage of the Northern armies in the final, decisive year of war. As early as August 1863 General Ulysses S. Grant and President Lincoln declared that the enlistment of black regiments was "the heaviest blow yet dealt to the rebellion." After the war was over, the influential New York *Tribune* said that the use of Negro troops had shortened the war by a year. The performance of black soldiers earned new respect for their race, made emancipation secure, and helped push the North toward a commitment to equality. The contribution of the Negro to the Union war effort created a debt that could be paid only by granting full citizenship to the race.

The drive for equal rights began in the North itself. Before the war, black men did not enjoy first-class citizenship in most Northern states. Several states had "black laws" that barred Negroes from immigration into the state, prohibited testimony by blacks against whites in courts, and otherwise discriminated against people with dark skin. In many parts of the North public accommodations, transportation facilities, hotels, and theaters were off-limits to Negroes. During the war black soldiers were thrown off the horse-drawn streetcars of Washington, Philadelphia, and New York on several occasions. Public schools in most parts of the North were segregated, and in some areas black children were barred from schools altogether. Blacks in Northern cities were frequently threatened by mob violence. In 1862 and 1863 white workingmen, fearful that emancipation would bring a horde of freedmen northward to compete for jobs, killed scores of Negroes in several urban race riots, climaxed by the New York Draft Riots of July 1863.

But the impetus of emancipation and the reputation of black soldiers began to break down racial discrimination in the North. Blacks were admitted to Congressional galleries and to White House receptions for the first time in 1864. A Negro lawyer was granted a license to present cases before the Supreme Court of the United States in 1865, just eight years after Roger B. Taney, as Chief Justice, had declared, in the Dred Scott decision, that black men had no rights that white men were bound to respect. Congress passed a series of laws forbidding discrimination against Negroes in the federal courts, the post office department, and on Washington streetcars. Northern states with "black laws" repealed them during, or shortly after, the war. In the postwar decades many states took even greater steps toward equal rights. Massachusetts passed a public accommodations law in 1865. Several other states followed suit in the 1870s and 1880s. Most Northern states abolished *de jure* school segregation. This equalitarian legislation was honored more in the breach than in practice, and a great deal of discrimination remained in the North despite the laws, but at least a beginning was made.

The question of Negro suffrage became the major issue of Reconstruction. The right to vote is a basic right of citizenship in a democracy, and the issue of black voters, especially in the South, where Negroes were a majority of the population in three states and a minority of more than 40 per cent in three others, generated more conflict, controversy, and dissension than any other single question in the fifteen years after the Civil War. By the end of 1865, most members of the Radical wing of the Republican party were committed to some kind of effort to secure equal voting rights for the freedmen; and by 1867, the moderate majority of the party had also come around to this position.

The prospect of Negro suffrage presented a good many practical difficulties. The four million freedmen were for the most part illiterate, penniless, and totally without political experience. The institution of slavery had crippled the self-reliance, initiative, pride, and manhood of many Negroes. The black people emerging from slavery did not have the social, economic, and educational resources to make themselves the instant equals of their old masters.

Although Radical Republicans were concerned about these problems, most of them suppressed their doubts and emphasized the positive arguments for Negro suffrage as a cornerstone of Reconstruction. The very logic of the Union war effort seemed to require the granting of equal citizenship to the Negro, who had fought not only for his own freedom but for the cause of the North. To have sloughed off these important allies into second-class citizenship would have been a repudiation of the debt that many people thought the Union owed the black man. Moreover, as a practical matter, it became clear that the freedmen would need the ballot to protect their basic civil rights. Republicans feared that if emancipated slaves were left without political power they would be reduced to some form of quasi-slavery or serfdom. The "black codes" passed by most Southern states in the months after the war confirmed this fear. Some of these codes required the arrest of black vagrants (the question of vagrancy to be determined by white sheriffs) and their lease for specified periods of time to white planters, apprenticed black children to white "masters" in certain circumstances, prohibited Negroes in some states from buying or renting land, or in other ways fastened a subordinate legal status upon the freedmen. The black codes presented the Radicals with dramatic evidence of the need for federal protection and political rights for the freedmen.

Many Republicans also feared that if the Southern states were readmitted to the Union without Negro suffrage, they would send Democratic congressmen to Washington and reduce the Republican party once again to a minority party. Thus the ballot for freedmen became something of a political necessity for the Republicans. But it was not only expediency or partisanship that motivated Republican thinking on this issue. Most Southern Democrats and a sizable proportion of their Northern brethren had been Confederates or Confederate sympathizers. They had fought a bitter war to destroy the Union and preserve slavery, causing 350,000 Northern deaths. Thus it was easy, and not entirely specious, for Northern Republicans (and most Northern voters) to identify the Democratic party with treason and the Republican party with union and freedom. The Northern mood of 1865–69 would not stand for any policy that readmitted the Democratic South to the Union with undiminished political power, thereby "letting the fruits of victory slip from our grasp." In such circumstances, the enfranchisement of the freedmen (who were expected, with good reason, to vote Republican) was patriotic as well as good politics for the Republicans.

There was also a punitive motive for Negro suffrage. Many Northerners, bitter toward "traitors" and "rebels," wanted to destroy the political basis of the Southern "aristocracy" they believed had caused the war and punish the Confederates by temporarily disfranchising them and permanently enfranchising their former slaves, thereby destroying the old political power structure of the South and creating a new Republican coalition of unionist whites and black freedmen.

Thus, for a variety of reasons, including equalitarianism, patriotism, political partisanship, and bitterness, the Radical wing of the Republican party pushed for enfranchisement of the freedmen as the cornerstone of their Reconstruction policy. In some cases this required political courage by Republicans who represented districts where racism was still a potent force. Despite the changes in Northern attitudes toward the Negro caused by the war, latent, and often overt, prejudice was still widespread. Blacks could not vote in most Northern states at the end of the war; many white voters, in spite of their hatred of the South, disliked the prospect of black equality and feared that freedmen's suffrage would be a major step toward equal rights in the North as well as in the South. For this reason, as well as their skepticism about the freedmen's qualifications for the ballot, moderate Republicans (a majority in the party) shied away from Negro suffrage in 1865–66 and tried to find a middle ground between black enfranchisement and readmission of the South with no federal protection at all for the freedmen. Their solution was the Fourteenth Amendment to the Constitution, proposed in 1866, which guaranteed citizenship and civil rights to the freedmen and reduced the representation of Southern states in Congress by the proportion of their adult male citizens who could not vote. Thus the South's political power was reduced, while an inducement was offered for voluntary enfranchisement of the freedmen.

This moderate proposal was sabotaged by President Andrew Johnson and by the short-sighted intransigence of the South. Johnson was a Tennessee Democrat, who remained loyal to the Union during the war and was rewarded with the 1864 vice-presidential nomination of the "Union Party," a wartime coalition of Republicans and War Democrats. After Lincoln's assassination, Johnson gradually gravitated back to his Democratic allegiance, urged the readmission of the Southern states with minimum conditions, and defied the policy of the Republican majority in Congress. With remarkable political ineptitude, Johnson vetoed moderate Congressional legislation, encouraged the Southern states to refuse ratification of the Fourteenth Amendment, alienated the moderate Republicans, and drove them closer to the Radical wing of the party. In the 1866 Congressional elections the Northern voters overwhelmingly repudiated Johnson's policies and gave the Republicans a mandate to push through their Reconstruction program over the President's vetoes.

In the spring of 1867, Congress passed a series of Reconstruction Acts that provided for military administration of the South until new state constitutions could be drawn up instituting universal manhood suffrage. Only after the state governments elected under these constitutions had ratified the Fourteenth Amendment would their representatives be readmitted to Congress. By the end of 1868, eight of the former Confederate states had been restored to the Union under these conditions; in 1869 Congress adopted the Fifteenth Amendment, prohibiting voting discrimination on grounds of race, and required the remaining three Southern states to ratify it before returning to the Union. By 1870, all the ex-Confederate states were under Republican control, with several black officeholders; the Fourteenth and Fifteenth Amendments were in the Constitution; the Union was restored; and the third Northern war aim of equality was achieved.

Or was it? Despite appearances, Radical Reconstruction rested on a weak foundation. During the 1870s the foundation gradually crumbled, and the walls came tumbling down. The framework of the Fourteenth and Fifteenth Amendments remained in the Constitution, to become the basis for the Negro Revolution of the mid-twentieth century; but in the 1870s the nation failed to carry out the promises of equality contained in these amendments.

There were several reasons for this failure. In the first place, most Northern whites were only superficially committed to the equalitarian purposes of Reconstruction, and many were openly hostile. From 1865 to 1869 there was a temporary radicalization of Northern public opinion that made possible the passage of Reconstruction measures enfranchising the freedmen, but this was the result more of war-born anti-southern sentiment than of genuine pro-Negro feeling. In 1867, when the Reconstruction Acts instituted Negro suffrage in the South, black men could vote in only seven of the twenty Northern states and in none of the four border states. Several times, from 1865 to 1868, Northern voters rejected Negro suffrage amendments to their own state constitutions. Not until the Fifteenth Amendment went into effect in 1870, three years after the Southern freedmen had been enfranchised, did most Negroes in the North have the right to vote. This Northern hostility or indifference to equal rights betokened ill success for an equalitarian Reconstruction policy, which required a strong national commitment if it was to succeed.

A second reason for the failure of Reconstruction was the bitter, sometimes violent, and always well-organized opposition of most Southern whites. Confederate veterans, accustomed to the use of violence to attain political ends, formed such organizations as the Ku Klux Klan, the White League, the Red Shirts, and numerous "rifle clubs" to terrorize Republicans, especially black Republicans, as a means of breaking down and destroying the party in the South. The federal government made several efforts between 1870 and 1874 to enforce equal rights against this Southern counterrevolution. The "Ku Klux Act" of 1871 gave the President sweeping powers to use the armed forces and courts to suppress white terrorist organizations; and this law, when enforced vigorously in 1871–72, was successful in temporarily quelling Southern anti-Republican violence. But a combination of factors after 1873 caused a decline in federal enforcement efforts: Financial depression, which diverted national attention to economic issues; Democratic victory in the Congressional elections of 1874; adverse Supreme Court decisions that stripped enforcement legislation of much of its power; and growing Northern disillusionment with the whole experiment of Reconstruction, which produced diminishing enthusiasm among Republicans for the party's Southern policy. Actually, even with the best of intentions, the federal government could not have completely suppressed the Ku Klux Klan and its sister organizations, since the number of troops in the army was inadequate for the purpose and most of the regiments were on the frontier fighting Indians.

Another dimension of Southern white resistance was the refusal or inability of many property-owning whites (and whites owned most of the property) to pay taxes to the "alien" Republican state governments. During Reconstruction most of the Southern states built public school systems almost from scratch, constructed new charitable and welfare institutions, and undertook ambitious programs of railroad building, aided by state grants and loans. All of this cost money, more money than the South had been accustomed to paying for public and social services, more than property owners were willing or able to pay in taxes, especially when they were opposed, as some of them were, to such innovations as public schools or when they believed that much of the revenue went into the pockets of corrupt officials. The Southern state governments, in some cases, were too weak or unstable to compel payment of taxes, and the resulting deficits were another reason for the collapse of Republican regimes as the 1870s wore on.

A third reason for the failure of Reconstruction was the illiteracy, inexperience, and poverty of the freedmen. It had been illegal to teach slaves (and free blacks, in some states) to read or write. The institution of slavery trained black people to dependence and denied them the opportunities and responsibilities of freedom. It would have been criminal of the North merely to emancipate the slaves, give them equal rights on paper, and then say: "All right, you're on your own—root hog, or die." And to the credit of some Northern people and the federal government, efforts were made to educate and assist the freedmen in their difficult transition from slavery to freedom. In one of the major outpourings of idealism and missionary zeal in American history, freedmen's aid societies in the North sent thou-

sands of teachers to the South to bring literacy to the
Negroes. The federal government created the Freedmen's
Bureau in 1865. More than a thousand freedmen's schools,
supported by Northern philanthropy and aided by the
Bureau, were in operation by 1870; and the new public
school system of the South was built on the foundation
provided by these mission schools. After 1870, the missionary societies concentrated their efforts on secondary
schools and colleges to train the teachers, ministers, and
leaders of the new black generation. The major institutions
of higher learning for Negroes evolved out of these freedmen's schools: Howard, Fisk, and Atlanta Universities;
Morehouse, Spelman, and Talladega Colleges; Hampton
Institute; Meharry Medical College; and many others. But
despite the admirable efforts of the crusade for freedmen's
education, 70 per cent of Southern blacks were still illiterate
in 1880. An effective crash program to educate and train
four million freed slaves would have required a far greater
commitment of national resources than was undertaken.
The mission societies did their best; but after the expiration
of the Freedmen's Bureau in 1870, they received no more
federal aid. Black Southerners remained at a large educational disadvantage in their relations with white Southerners.

Another facet of the black man's disadvantage was his
poverty. Most emancipated slaves owned little more than
the clothes on their backs when freedom came. Unless they
received some kind of massive economic assistance, it was
clear they would remain an economically subordinate class,
dependent on whites for employment. Many abolitionists
and Radical Republicans believed that there must be an
economic reconstruction of the South if civil and political
reconstruction were to succeed. The great abolitionist
orator, Wendell Phillips, Congressman Thaddeus Stevens,
and others urged the adoption of a thorough program of
land reform as a basis of Reconstruction. They called for

the confiscation of plantations owned by former Confederates, and the redistribution of the land in forty-acre plots to the freedmen. But this proposal threatened the sanctity of private property as a basis of society and was too radical for most Northerners. A small amount of Confederate property was expropriated during the war, and some of these lands found their way to black ownership; but there was no major program of agrarian reform. Most blacks became wage-earners, sharecroppers, or tenant farmers, rather than independent, landowning farmers. The South was not reconstructed economically, and consequently political reconstruction rested on an unstable foundation.

Because of educational and economic disadvantages, black people lacked the social and psychological resources to sustain their equal rights in the face of Southern white counterrevolution. This is not to deny that there were effective Negro leaders during Reconstruction. In fact, one of the remarkable things about the era was that this largely uneducated and propertyless people could produce such a group of able leaders. Twenty black men were elected to the national House of Representatives and two to the Senate after the war. Several Negroes served as lieutenant governors, secretaries of state, superintendents of education, and treasurers of Southern states. No black man was elected governor, but one Negro lieutenant-governor, Pinckney B. S. Pinchback, served for a month as acting Governor of Louisiana. Blanche K. Bruce was an outstanding black senator from Mississippi; Robert B. Elliott, of South Carolina, and John R. Lynch, of Mississippi, were talented black congressmen. These men and others provided strong leadership for their race, but they could not overcome the determined white power structure. At least 100,000 black veterans of the Union army lived in the South during Reconstruction. Republican state governors enrolled many of them in state militia regiments to protect the freedmen's rights against terrorism. But there were four or five times as many white veterans of the Confederate army in the South, many of them enrolled in the Ku Klux Klan and similar organizations. These men were better armed and better led than the black militiamen; and in the pitched battles of the violence-wracked years of Reconstruction, the white para-military groups usually prevailed.

One other major reason for the failure of Reconstruction was the instability of the coalition called the Republican Party in the South. This coalition was composed of a small number of Northern whites ("carpetbaggers"), Southern whites ("scalawags"), and the freedmen. Some of the carpetbaggers and scalawags deserved the pejorative connotations of these words, invented by their opponents, but others were honest, sincere men who wanted to make interracial democracy work. Inevitably there was friction among the three components of the Republican coalition. Native white Republicans shared some of the region's dislike for "outsiders," and there were power struggles within the Republican Party that pitted carpetbagger against scalawag. Though blacks provided most of the Republican votes, whites held most of the offices, which produced a growing demand by Negro leaders for greater representation and power in party councils. Many scalawags could not transcend their Southern upbringing and were uncomfortable in a predominantly black party, especially when blacks tried to move into positions of power. Some of the carpetbaggers also had difficulty transcending deeply ingrained racial prejudices. The Southern Democrats, increasingly united and strong under the banner of "home rule and white supremacy," took advantage of racial and other tensions in the Republican Party, and, by a combination of inducements and threats, brought many scalawags over from the "black Republicans" to the "white man's party." The unstable Republican coalition broke into sqabbling factions in several Southern states in the 1870s, making it easier for the Democrats, aided by the terrorization of black voters, to gain control of one state after another.

How did the North react to crumbling Republican power in the South? Many Northerners had hoped that with the passage of the Reconstruction Acts and adoption of the Fourteenth and Fifteenth Amendments, the task of restoring the South to the Union and ensuring equal rights would be completed. The North wanted to turn its attention to other issues. As reports of corruption, conflict, and violence filtered up from the South, however, it was clear that Reconstruction was not yet accomplished, and that continuous and vigorous national effort would be required to maintain Negro rights against Southern counterrevolution. But disillusionment and indifference sapped the Northern will. As early as 1870, Horace Greeley's New York *Tribune*, which had been one of the foremost advocates of Radical Reconstruction a few years earlier, declared that it was time to "have done with Reconstruction. The country is sick of it." In the 1870s, *The Nation*, an independent liberal weekly with great influence among Northern intellectuals, became increasingly disenchanted with the results of Negro suffrage. *The Nation* declared that the Republican state governments of South Carolina and Louisiana were "a gang of robbers making war on civilization and morality," and concluded that the average black man "as regards the right performance of a voter's duty is as ignorant as a horse or a sheep." By 1876, *The Nation* had decided that the North should never have attempted "the insane task of making newly-emancipated field hands, led by barbers and barkeepers, fancy they knew as much about government and were as capable of administering it, as the whites."

Many Northern journalists visited the South during the 1870s and wrote feature stories that were increasingly sympathetic to the white viewpoint. James Shepherd Pike, a reporter for the New York *Tribune*, gathered his articles into a book published in 1874 with the title *The Prostrate State: South Carolina Under Negro Government*. This book and others portrayed a South ruled and ruined by "Carpet-bag-Negro government." Under the impact of this journalistic barrage, Northern public opinion gradually became indifferent, and even hostile, to the plight of freedmen and Republicans in the South. There was a growing consensus that Reconstruction was a mistake, that the federal government ought to cease its "misguided efforts" to enforce equal rights in the South, and that the Southern people should be left alone to work out the race problem on their own terms. "The whole public are tired of these annual autumnal outbreaks in the South," wrote the United States Attorney General, in refusing a request from the Republican Governor of Mississippi for federal troops to protect Negro voters in 1875. Mississippi was captured by the Democrats in the election, and the Attorney General's remark symbolized Northern indifference to this development.

Widespread reports of Republican corruption, incompetence, and misgovernment were one of the most important factors in turning Northern opinion against Reconstruction. It would be foolish to deny that there was corruption in the South. Like all myths, the myth of greedy, rapacious carpetbaggers, jackal-like scalawags, and incompetent, bribe-taking black politicians is based on a modicum of truth. But reality bore only slight relation to the grotesque picture depicted by contemporary journalists and echoed by many historians. Disorder and mistakes inevitably accompany rapid social change such as occurred in the postwar South. The building of railroads, the construction of a public school system, the physical rehabilitation of a region scarred by war, and the democratization of the Southern political system could not have been achieved without a dislocation of values and standards. And the Southern situation should be placed in national perspective. The post–Civil War era was an age of corruption, bribery, and swindling in Northern as well as Southern states and in the federal government itself. All the Southern state governments combined probably did not steal as much from the public treasury as the Tweed Ring in New York City. Even the South Carolina and Louisiana legislatures could scarcely match the brazen bribery that took place in Albany, New York. One contemporary critic charged that the Standard Oil Company could do anything it wanted with the Pennsylvania legislature except refine it.

Despite the propaganda of Southern whites, it was not so much dishonest Republican government that they opposed as it was any Republican government at all, honest or dishonest. The Reconstruction government of Mississippi was clean and honest, yet it, too, was overthrown by terror and intimidation. Why, then, did influential segments of Northern opinion accept the journalistic descriptions of Southern corruption? Primarily because the North, in spite of its superficially pro-Negro attitude of 1865–69, had never really been converted to a genuine belief in racial equality. The Northern radicalism of 1865–69 was produced mainly by war-born hatred for Southern whites and temporary gratitude to black soldiers who had fought for the Union, but as the memories and passions of war faded in the 1870's the underlying racism of the North reasserted itself. Thus the Northern people were willing to believe exaggerated stories of the incompetence and corruption of "Negro-Carpetbag" governments. As the 1876 centennial of American independence approached there was a movement toward sectional reconciliation and a rededication to national unity. This was all very well, but the freedmen became victims of this "clasping of hands across the bloody chasm." The price of reconciliation was "home rule" for the South and a cessation of Northern interference in Southern "domestic affairs."

With the exception of some of the old Radical Republicans and abolitionists still alive in 1876, the North was prepared to retreat from Reconstruction. It was a Presidential election year, and all signs pointed to a Democratic victory. Capitalizing on the economic depression, widespread disgust with the scandals of the Grant administration, and disillusionment with Reconstruction, Democrats hoped to expand their 1874 capture of the House of Representatives into occupation of the White House. The disputed Presidential election of 1876 resulted in one of the most bizarre political crises of American history. Democrat Samuel J. Tilden won a majority of the popular vote, and was only one electoral vote short of victory, with the outcome in the three Southern states still controlled by Republicans—South Carolina, Florida, and Louisiana—in dispute. Two sets of electoral returns were submitted from each state. If Tilden won any of these votes, he was elected; Republican Rutherford B. Hayes needed the electoral votes of all three states to become the nineteenth President. With the Democratic House and Republican Senate deadlocked over the issue, there could be no Congressional counting of electoral votes, as specified by the Constitution. Passions ran high, many feared another civil war, and there was a real danger that no President would be inaugurated on March 4, 1877. Finally, Congress appointed a special commission to canvass the disputed votes. The commission, by a partisan vote, awarded all the electors to Hayes, thereby making him President. Angry Democrats in the House charged fraud and threatened a filibuster to prevent completion of the electoral count. Behind the scenes, however, several Southern Democrats were in consultation with Hayes's lieutenants, and a series of agreements was worked

out whereby the Southerners promised to allow a completion of the vote in return for commitments from Hayes
to withdraw the last federal troops from South Carolina
and Louisiana (where the federal presence was the only
power keeping duly elected Republican governments in
office), to give political patronage to Southern Democrats,
and to use his influence in behalf of appropriations for
Southern internal improvements. This "Compromise of
1877" ended the electoral crisis. Hayes took office and
promptly withdrew the troops from South Carolina and
Louisiana. The Republican governments immediately col-
lapsed and the South became solidly Democratic.

Some Republicans and former abolitionists charged that
the compromise was a sellout of the freedmen; in a sense
they were right. Hayes's withdrawal of the troops brought
an end to meaningful national efforts to enforce the Fourteenth and Fifteenth Amendments in the South until the
1950s. In the three decades after 1877, Southern blacks
were gradually disfranchised, Jim-Crowed, and reduced to
a degraded second-class citizenship. But Hayes really had
had no choice in 1877. Democrats controlled the House
and threatened to block appropriations if he tried to use
the army in the South; the North had already given up its
moral commitment to Reconstruction; and the overthrow
of Southern Republican governments was a virtual *fait
accompli* by the time Hayes took office.

The Civil War and Reconstruction, therefore, were a
revolution *manqué*. The Union was restored and the slaves
freed, but the Negro did not achieve equality. There was
a period of bright promise in the late 1860s, but it flickered
out in the backlash of the 1870s. A genuine revolution of
equality would have required a revolution in institutions
and attitudes which did not occur. Despite the enfranchisement of the freedmen, the basic institutional structure of
Southern society remained unchanged: The whites retained

most of the wealth, property, education, power, and experience. The racial attitudes of both North and South bent just enough to accept (sometimes reluctantly) emancipation, but remained basically opposed to genuine equality. The revolution of racial equality was a failure.

And yet not quite a failure. The Civil War–Reconstruction era produced the system of public schools and private colleges for Negroes that brought literacy to the race and trained future generations of leaders. From the colleges founded by Northern abolitionists and missionaries after the war were graduated, among others, W. E. B. DuBois, Walter White, Thurgood Marshall, Martin Luther King, James Farmer, and Stokely Carmichael. The Fourteenth and Fifteenth Amendments were permanent results of Reconstruction, and in our own time the fusion of educated black leadership and reinvigoration of these Amendments has generated a Second Reconstruction that may produce the racial equality envisaged by the first.

4. LOUIS R. HARLAN

Booker T. Washington and the National Negro Business League

White America did not abruptly abandon the goals of Reconstruction. The process began before the removal of the last troops from the South in 1877 and continued into this century. Throughout the 1880s the status of the Southern Negro remained ambiguous. Although racial prejudice was pervasive and various forms of segregation existed, the rigid structure of Jim Crow had not yet been established, and inconsistency characterized racial mores. Intimidation, fraud, and coercion limited Negro political activity; but large numbers of blacks continued to vote, and for two decades after Reconstruction many black politicians retained their hold on minor offices. Until 1901 Southern constituencies sent black men to Congress. However, during these years the enactment of Jim Crow laws, forcing segregation of the races in public accommodations and transportation facilities, gradually spread throughout the South; and the chaotic decade of the 1890s brought the total "capitulation to racism."

Between 1890 and 1910, Southern whites effectively disfranchised Negroes and drew a rigid "color line." This assault upon the Negro's civil rights was only one aspect of a mounting wave of white aggression against black America. Violence dominated the period. More than two thousand blacks were lynched between 1890 and 1910, and cities in both the North and the South were the scene of vicious anti-Negro riots culminating in the "Red Summer" of 1919.

Although Negroes continued to protest the deterioration of their position in American life, the dominant trend in Negro thought—particularly among Southern Negroes—emphasized accommodation, racial solidarity, and self-help. The man whose racial ideology epitomized these ideas and who dominated the era was Booker T. Washington.

Born a slave, then educated at Hampton Institute, Washington served most of his adult life as head of Tuskegee Institute. From this position, he became the leading advocate of vocational education for black Americans, and gained national notoriety for his speech at the Atlanta Exposition in 1895, in which he called upon Negroes to forswear politics and accept disfranchisement while concentrating on building the economic foundation for eventual integration into American life.

Immensely respected by whites and the mass of Negroes, Washington was not without opponents, and his racial leadership did not go unchallenged. Anti-Bookerite sentiments were centered in the North and strongest among black intellectuals, who were, for the most part, products of the leading Northern universities. The most prominent of these "radicals"—as the opponents of Washington were called—was W. E. B. DuBois. Born in Massachusetts and educated at Fisk University and Harvard, DuBois taught classics, history, and sociology at Atlanta University, and later served as editor of The Crisis, the militant organ of the National Association for the Advancement of Colored People.

Early in his career DuBois had cooperated with Washington, and the two men shared many values and attitudes; but the publication in 1903 of the essay, "Of Booker T. Washington and Others," in DuBois's The Souls of Black Folk marked the open break between these two leaders.

In this essay, DuBois criticized the paradox involved in Washington's "programme of industrial education, conciliation of the South, and submission and silence as to civil and political rights." Without the vote, "civic equality," and a liberally educated leadership, racial progress and even self-defense became impossible.

DuBois's emphasis on militant protest led to the Niagara Movement and eventually, in 1909, to the formation of the NAACP. At the same time, the conflict between Washington and DuBois took on many of the aspects of a sectarian dispute, doctrinal at its core, but at the same time highly personal; and much of DuBois's criticism was directed at the way in which the "Tuskegee Machine" attempted to silence its opponents.

Until quite recently, few historians have been able to write about this period without siding with either Washington or DuBois on these matters. The result has been the development of stereotypes which present a unidimensional Washington, either in the guise of the consummate racial statesman or a fawning Uncle Tom. DuBois has been better understood, but usually his thought has been viewed by friend and foe as uniformly radical. Focusing on the National Negro Business League, one of the main institutional supports of Washington's "Tuskegee Machine," Professor Louis R. Harlan of the University of Maryland reveals the many ambiguities and complexities in the relationship between Washington and DuBois and the ways in which simple stereotypes can cloud our understanding of the past.

SINCE the death of the great Negro conservative leader Booker T. Washington in 1915, there has been such a tremendous reorientation of Negro social thought that we have tended to read Negro history backward. That is,

we have tended to find, in the past, spokesman for our
present ideas—our own conventional wisdom—contesting
with spokesmen for the now repudiated conventional wisdom of the past. Historians looking back a half-century
have discovered there the accommodationist Washington
and his allies, mostly whites, locked in mortal combat with
W. E. B. DuBois and his militant "Talented Tenth." A
total war between the powers of light and darkness, with
DuBois on the side of light. This simplistic view is now
being re-examined by a number of scholars, who find consensus as well as conflict in the Negro social thought of
the turn of the century. As August Meier has pointed out,
in his excellent book, *Negro Thought in America, 1880–
1915,* Washington and DuBois, born twelve years apart,
were products of the same age and, to a considerable extent,
shared underlying assumptions. Both were products of a
nineteenth-century education; and at the turn of the century
both looked backward in different ways to nineteenth-century ideals. This essay may, it is hoped, contribute in a minor
way to the dispassionate examination of Negro thought in
the Progressive Era by exploring one idea that DuBois
and Washington shared: the idea of Negro business enterprise as a means of advancement for the race. Let me say
in advance that it is not my intention to disparage DuBois,
whose ideas changed radically after 1900. He was ever
learning, searching for the truth, even when the trail led
to China. Further, I have not attempted a systematic study
of the actual condition of Negro business, which has been
fully treated by other scholars.

The idea of the National Negro Business League was
born in the brain of W. E. B. DuBois, but it was Washington who took the idea and made of it an institution,
an important part of the so-called "Tuskegee Machine."
In 1899, a year before Washington took up the idea,
DuBois sponsored an Atlanta University conference on

"The Negro in Business," and was a member of the committee which drafted the conference proposal for "the organization in every town and hamlet where the colored people dwell, of Negro Business Men's Leagues, and the gradual federation from these of state and national organizations." The Atlanta professor expressed not only the organizational idea of the Business League but also its general social outlook. Reiterating the Negro nationalist cry of "Negro money for Negro merchants," he deplored the shortage of Negro businessmen and business institutions, which gave the race "a one-sided development" and put it "out of sympathy with the industrial and mercantile spirit of the age." It is clear that DuBois himself was very much in sympathy with the *Zeitgeist* of a commercial age. At the 1899 meeting of the Afro-American Council he was made director of a bureau on Negro business, with the duty of organizing business leagues. As a social scientist, rather than an action leader, he began by gathering statistical information and drafting organizational plans.

When Booker T. Washington called the organizational meeting of the National Negro Business League in the summer of 1900, he was accused by DuBois and his friends in Boston, Chicago, and elsewhere of stealing the idea and of dividing the Negro ranks by creating a new organization outside the Afro-American Council, "a new organization of which he will be president, moderator and dictator," as the Chicago *Conservator* put it. At the 1899 meeting of the Afro-American Council, which Washington refused to attend, the *Conservator* said, "he had ample opportunity to suggest plans along business lines and Prof. DuBois, the most scholarly and one of the most conservative members of the Council, who is chairman of the Business Bureau would have been glad to receive Mr. Washington's co-operation." Washington gave no public attention to these criticisms, nor ever acknowledged any

debt to DuBois for the idea of the Business League, though
he occasionally quoted from DuBois's 1899 report. Washington insisted that the idea had come from his tours all
over the country, where he had found many successful
Negro businessmen living isolated and unsung, and that
he had organized the Business League in order to give
publicity to their achievements and to help them help
themselves. Nevertheless, Washington's secretary, Emmett
J. Scott, wrote to the editor of the *Conservator* that Washington was "not especially concerned as to the matter of
leadership," that he did not seek to "throw obstacles in
the path of any organization working in the interest of his
people," and that he was creating a separate business organization because "its attention will not be divided as
between sociological and other such questions. . . ." And
Washington himself made a point of attending the next
Afro-American Council meeting, to confront his critics.
By 1903, the Afro-American Council had been destroyed
by the intensity of its internal dissensions, and the Washingtonian H. T. Kealing was able to say that "the Sage of
Tuskegee had a long and true vision. He also knew the
value of singlemindedness and the danger of hydraheaded-
ness, so he went ahead. The event now justifies his pre-
science, for the Afro-American Council is dead and the
Business League is at the period of its greatest activity.
Success is the best witness wisdom can have."

The 300 businessmen and other Washington supporters
who gathered at Boston in 1900 "to take stock" faced a
crisis in race relations, and Washington moved forcefully,
and even brutally, to control their response to this crisis.
Just before and during the meeting, the papers were full
of news of race riots in New Orleans, New York, and
Akron. These events, Emmett Scott later said, "painted a
sombre picture of racial friction and planted in the hearts
of many the seeds of dark despair." And yet, in the two

days and nights of the conference, "there was not one single reference to the riots or to the conditions that gave rise to them," Washington later reported with pride. "These were business men, come to Boston for a definite purpose with which politics had no connection, and they attended strictly to business." Washington and "the powers that governed the Business League," to maintain this unanimity, prevented a delegation of New Bedford, Massachusetts, businessmen from rendering their report, for fear that it would "deal with topics which were forbidden at that gathering." One New Bedford delegate was still angry two years later, when he wrote to Emmett Scott:

They knew we [the New Bedford delegation] were all members of the Union League . . . and they knew we were accustomed to speak out. But their fears and suspicions were unjustified, not a word in our report but dealt with business pure and simple. We did not agree with Mr. Washington's fiat (with the New Orleans horror and the Georgia outrages still burning in our memories) but we respected the wishes of the callers of the meeting and laid supreme questions of manhood by, for the sordid materialism of business, although our hearts throbbed in unison with that lofty, manly sentiment of Emerson's
"For what avail the plough or sail,
"Or land, or life, if FREEDOM fail."

Possibly to allay criticism, Washington brought William Lloyd Garrison, son of the abolitionist, to speak. "The particular word I wish to leave with you is this: Aim to be your own employers," said Garrison. "If the title deeds to the land of the South were in the hands of the colored people, there would be no Negro problem, but, instead, a very large white one."

The National Negro Business League grew rapidly, the 300 delegates of 1900 swelling to some 3,000 when the national convention returned to Boston in 1915, the year of Washington's death. By 1915, there were about 600

local leagues, of which approximately 300 had been organized and chartered by the national league. Membership
was estimated at anywhere from 5,000 to 40,000, in thirty-
six states and West Africa. The organization remained
under the tight control of the Tuskegeean. Though not
himself a business man, Washington remained the president throughout his life, and his successor at Tuskegee,
Robert R. Moton, also became head of the Business League.
The corresponding secretary of the Business League, until
1922, was Washington's private secretary, Emmett J. Scott.
A succession of national organizers—Fred R. Moore,
Ralph W. Tyler, Charles R. Moore, and Albon W. Holsey
—spent their time largely in Northern cities, stimulating
or reviving local business leagues, thus keeping the head-
quarters in the small Alabama town in touch with the
leading centers of Negro enterprise.

Financial records of the Business League are incomplete,
but they make clear that the businessmen's organization
was not affluent enough to finance itself. Life memberships,
at $25 each, reached about a hundred by 1915; but the
League was about $500 in debt to Tuskegee Institute; and
in 1916 it got out of debt at a cost of $1,500, thanks to
a gift from Julius Rosenwald. The private correspondence
of the national organizers indicates that many of the local
leagues were largely on paper, reviving each year to send
delegates to the national meeting, or torn by schisms and
leadership struggles. Nevertheless, the Business League was
strong enough during Washington's lifetime to be the
organizational center of Negro conservatism. The businessmen held the center of the stage at the annual meetings,
but the League absorbed the Washingtonian lawyers, doc-
tors, educators, and other professional people after the
collapse of the Afro-American Council. Affiliated with it
were a Negro press association, bar association, and similar
organizations of bankers, insurance men, undertakers, and

retail merchants. In every community the local business league gave conservatives a rallying point against the militants organized in suffrage leagues, the Niagara Movement, and the NAACP. The Richmond Business League gave Washington a forum there during the Virginia disfranchisement convention in 1901; the "Boston Riot" of 1903 occurred at a meeting sponsored by the Boston businessmen.

The National Negro Business League was significant not only as a help to Washington in the Negro leadership struggle, but also as a promoter of Negro enterprise and as an expression of Washington's social outlook. The League unabashedly presented the case for a segregated Negro economy and the exaltation of Negro businessmen to a high place parallel to that of white businessmen. The annual meetings never systematically analyzed the status, problems, and opportunities of Negro business. Instead, the meetings were given over almost entirely to highly personal accounts by businessmen of their "ups and downs," ending with Horatio Alger formulas for business success. Since plain men of business were seldom natural orators, however, the "life of the meeting" was Washington himself, who conducted the "quizzing" of the speakers. By propounding leading questions at the close of a paper or talk, Washington and other "quizzers" from the floor extracted information and homilies that would otherwise not have come to the surface. As one delegate facetiously put it, " 'The Wizard' thus compels a man to make a good speech whether he knows how or not." All these colloquies were taken down by a stenographer and published in the annual reports, allegedly as objective evidence of Negro business progress.

At the local level, the League members stimulated small retail businesses, through "buy black" campaigns, to persuade people to "pass by the Dago store, the German establishment, the Irish institution, and give their trade and

spend their money with their own struggling people. . . ."
Scott organized a Negro business service to advise and aid
small businesses, but it seems to have died through lack
of support. Although there was much talk of Negro millionaires and Negro trusts, the League never seriously grappled
with the real problems of Negro business: Lack of capital,
because poorly paid Negroes had small savings, and because white bankers refused to lend to or invest in Negro
enterprises; lack of a business tradition among Negroes
recently out of slavery, so that few Negroes had the chance
to grow up in a business, and most successful Negro businessmen educated their children, not for business, but for
professions; the virtual impossibility of a successful Negro
economy, because of the narrowness of a market confined
to Negroes of low average income; and, finally, the perilous
condition of all small business in an age of mass production, giant corporations, and chain stores.

It seems a legitimate question why Washington was so
involved in a business organization, since he was an educator. Part of the answer is that he was more a businessman
than he seemed to be. His role as principal of Tuskegee
was somewhat entrepreneurial, in that he used the capital
of philanthropy and the cheap labor of students to build
a one-room school into a multimillion-dollar educational
enterprise; and in the early years Tuskegee sold everything
from bricks to buggies in the local market. Even before
Andrew Carnegie's large personal gift to him in 1903,
Washington's personal property in land, residences, and
business buildings gave him a rental income of nearly $100
a month. He also owned stock in a Birmingham coal company, $500 of stock in a Massachusetts shoe company,
$600 of stock in the Tuskegee Cotton Oil Company, a
secret investment in at least two Negro newspapers and
a magazine, and, probably, stock in Negro cotton mills
and oil mills in which he took an active interest. At Tus-

kegee Institute were a savings bank, to encourage thrift on the campus, and the Southern Improvement Company, with philanthropic capital to encourage Negro land ownership by selling on long terms at low interest. Washington was actually a bigger businessman than any but a handful of the members of the Business League.

Washington's interest in the Business League also stemmed from his evolutionary approach to the race problem. The Progressive Era was, paradoxically, an era of retrogression for the Negro, when political proscription was accompanied by racial violence all over the nation, and followed by segregation and discrimination more extreme than ever before. The recent scholarship of C. Vann Woodward, Rayford Logan, and others attributes these developments to economic depression and political turmoil in the South, Darwinistic racialism and imperialism, and a strangely *laissez-faire* attitude of the federal government during the age of reform. To Washington, however, as to most of his contemporaries, the Negro's worsening position seemed to result from the reaction of whites against pushing the Negro into positions for which he was unready. Washington expressed this view in 1909 in these words:

He [the Negro] came out of slavery with the idea that somehow or other the Government, which freed him, was going to support and protect him, and that the great hope of his race was in politics and in the ballot. In the last decade the Negro has settled down to the task of building his own fortune and of gaining through thrift, through industry, and through business success that which he has been denied in other directions.

The gospel of thrift, industry, and property ownership had been instilled in Washington during his student years at Hampton Institute, where its founder, General Samuel C. Armstrong, gained a lifelong dominance over Washington's thought. Armstrong, the son of New England missionaries

in Hawaii, believed that Negroes, like that other "backward," or childlike, race, the Polynesians, were lazy and
shiftless, and that all of them needed to be sent to school
to learn the Calvinistic virtues of industry and thrift before
they would be ready for higher civilization. This viewpoint,
which underlay Washington's industrial curriculum at Tuskegee, was reinforced by his contacts with successful Northern businessmen during his fund-raising campaigns. The
advice of John Wanamaker and Andrew Carnegie—and
of Theodore Roosevelt too—was that Negroes needed to
get out of politics and get into business. There were "acres
of diamonds" all around the Negro, particularly in the
South, just awaiting an enterprising hand to gather them.

"Man may discriminate," said Washington, "but the
economic laws of trade and commerce cannot discriminate." A man of action, rather than an intellectual, Washington accepted the conventional economic ideas of his
time, the nineteenth-century climate of classical economics.
He thought that economic life and all men's economic
actions were controlled by natural laws, which men defied
at their peril. These perfect laws had no place for anything
so irrational as race prejudice. "When an individual pro-
duces what the world wants," Washington believed, "the
world does not stop long to inquire what is the color of
the skin of the producer." This article of faith ignored the
fact that, in reality, the world was very conscious of skin
color. To this black Polonius, it followed, as the night the
day, that whenever Negroes demonstrated the virtues of
good businessmen by getting property, nice houses with
several bedrooms, bank accounts, and property taxes, the
Southern whites who surrounded them would give them
the ballot, the Pullman berth, and other unspecified per-
quisites of full citizenship without a qualm. Northern whites
would likewise recognize proven ability and give Negroes
whatever place they had earned in their society.

In Washington's opinion, business success would gain white recognition of Negroes more surely than any other achievement; for the world measured men and races by "certain visible signs of civilization and strength," outward signs of an inward grace. Washington said:

As one goes through our Western states and sees the Scandinavians in Minnesota, for example, owning and operating nearly one-third of the farms in the state; and then as he goes through one of the cities of Minnesota and sees block after block of brick stores owned by these Scandinavians; as he sees factories and street railways owned and operated by these same people, and as he notes that as a rule, these people live in neat, well-kept cottages where there are refinement and culture, on nice streets, that have been paid for, he can't help but have confidence in and respect for such people, no matter how he has been educated to feel regarding them.

Through a thousand speeches extolling the business career for Negroes and promoting the Business League, Washington seemed to say that Negroes should turn away from the avenues of political action and civil rights agitation which, for the time being anyhow, were already blocked, and travel up the economic road to affluence and consequent economic strength. In this opportunism, he avoided complete acquiescence and accommodation by asserting that the economic approach would re-establish political and civil rights on a firmer basis, and thus provide a new emancipation. Washington illustrated this point with many dubious examples. He recounted the story of "Old Jim Hill," whose name was changed to "Mr. James Hill" after he had acquired property and a bank account. The celebrated Indianola, Mississippi, postmistress, whose post office the local whites forced President Theodore Roosevelt to close, was better off in the banking business with her husband, and even lent money to local whites. Washington alleged that, "almost without exception, whether in the North or

in the South, wherever I have seen a Negro who was succeeding in business, who was a taxpayer, a man who pos-
sessed intelligence and high moral character, that man was
treated with respect by the people of both races."

There was some ambiguity in Washington's attitude
toward the separate-economy concept. He always opposed
colonization schemes, either within or outside the United
States; he insisted that there was "no color line in eggs,"
and that natural resources knew nothing of skin color; and
he constantly harped on the effect that Negro success would
have on white attitudes. Nevertheless, he urged Negro businessmen to come South precisely because the chief market
for Negro business was among their own people, more of
whom were in the South than anywhere else in America.
The effect of segregation, he said, "has frequently been
to create for the Negro a special business opportunity."
Although he tried to keep Madame C. J. Walker, a wealthy
manufacturer of hair straightener, off the Business League
program, even though she was a life member and a donor
to many Negro causes, including Tuskegee, and although
he kept saloonkeepers out of the League on moral grounds,
even though they were a leading class of Negro businessmen, Washington recognized that the chief Negro business
opportunities lay in performing services that whites would
not perform and in marketing products designed for Negroes. And he showed particular fondness for such all-
Negro, segregated towns as Boley, Oklahoma, and Mound
Bayou, Mississippi, which the Business League declared
"the finest possible concrete argument that the negro is
ready for citizenship." In these self-segregated towns Negroes could enter naturally and easily into any occupations
for which their talents qualified them, Washington believed.
Hoping the Mound Bayou could become a model of Negro
enterprise, with a diversified economy parallel to that in
the white world, he persuaded Julius Rosenwald to invest

$25,000 in a $100,000 oil-mill enterprise at Mound Bayou, which soon failed, and he introduced Charles Banks of the Bank of Mound Bayou to a number of New York bankers in an effort to save that business concern. Washington ignored the fact that these segregated businesses and segregated towns gave Negro economic leaders a vested interest in segregation.

Washington's public optimism about Negro opportunities was not always borne out by his private correspondence. In 1904, for example, Negro businessmen who exemplified the qualities Washington extolled were molested in West Point, Mississippi. Isaiah T. Montgomery wrote him that:

> Thomas Harvey runs a neat little Grocery, he kept a Buggy and frequently rode to his place of business, he was warned to sell his Buggy and walk. Mr. Chandler keeps a Grocery, he was ordered to leave, but was finally allowed to remain on good behavior. Mr. Meacham ran a business and had a Pool Table in connection therewith, he was ordered to close up and don overalls for manual labor. Mr. Cook conducted a hack business between the Depots and about town, using two Vehicles, he was notified that he would be allowed to run only one and was ordered to sell the other.

A printer named Buchanan, also of West Point, had a piano in his home and allowed his daughter, who was his cashier and bookkeeper, to ride the family buggy to and from work, until "a mass meeting of whites decided that the mode of living practiced by the Buchanan family had a bad effect on the cooks and washerwomen, who aspired to do likewise, and became less disposed to work for the whites." A mob forced Buchanan's family to flee, during his absence, and refused to allow him back in town even to pack. So much for the economic panacea for Negro ills.

Although the Business League's heyday was a period of tremendous economic, social, and ideological readjustment for Negroes, the League and its exaltation of the business ideal met surprisingly little resistance before the First World War. One reason was that such white champions of Negro militancy as Oswald Garrison Villard and John E. Milholland also supported the Business League. By the 1920s, white and Negro leaders of the NAACP supported identification of the Negro with labor; but in Washington's day the alienation of Negro leaders from the lily-white unions was almost complete. What muted opposition there was to business leadership came from a minority of Negroes of the professional class. To understand their response, it may be helpful to employ the concept of the status revolution which Richard Hofstadter has used to interpret the Progressive Movement in the same period.

The industrial revolution of the nineteenth century, said Hofstadter, threw self-made industrial millionaires to the top of American society. The old elite of the Northeast—preachers, teachers, lawyers, and merchants—had no choice but ruin or subservience. In the Progressive Movement, members of this elite saw a chance to lead a popular movement which would restore them to their former status.

Application of this concept of the status revolution to the Negro professionals and their leadership of Negro militancy might prove fruitful, but in this essay only its relation to the thought of Washington and DuBois can be explored.

In an interesting article for *The Outlook*, in 1909, Washington noted that the political leaders of Black Reconstruction were "what may be called the aristocracy of the race," many of whom had been free, or practically free, before the Civil War. A number of them had been favored house servants or sons of their masters and were given special educational opportunities. After the war, while these leaders found scope for their talents in politics, in the professions, and in services catering to the white upper class, they and their descendants were also singled out by Northern philanthropy for higher education and professional training. For, in the nineteenth century, before the industrial *nouveaux riches* had assumed much social responsibility, the center of philanthropy was still in New England and among the old elite. The very Northern elements which were losing power attempted, through philanthropy, to create a Negro elite in their own image. While this older elite suffered loss of status through the withdrawal of suffrage and political offices and the loss of white patronage for their services there grew up what Washington referred to as "a middle class among the colored people," slaves before the war, but now becoming landowners, artisans, and businessmen. Washington identified himself with these self-made Negro men of enterprise; DuBois was never of them.

Although DuBois said in 1898 that "The day the Negro race courts and marries the savings-bank will be the day of its salvation," by 1903 he deplored many changes in Negro society. He wrote:

The old leaders of Negro opinion . . . are being replaced by new; neither the black preacher nor the black teacher leads as he did two decades ago. Into their places are pushing . . . the businessmen, all those with property and money. And with this change, so curiously parallel to that of the Other-world, goes too the same inevitable change in ideals. The South laments to-day the slow, steady disappearance of a certain type of Negro, —the faithful, courteous slave of other days, with his incorruptible honesty and dignified humility. He is passing away just as surely as the old type of Southern gentleman is passing, and from not dissimilar causes,—the sudden transformation of a fair far-off ideal of Freedom into the hard reality of bread-winning and the consequent deification of Bread.

What if to the Mammonism of America be added the rising Mammonism of the re-born South, and the Mammonism of this South be reinforced by the budding Mammonism of its half-awakened black millions?

If DuBois was a "radical" by 1903, he was clearly one who looked back nostalgically to an earlier society more to his liking. The early volumes of the *Crisis* under his editorship, however, indicate that he had not rejected capitalism. Its columns of racial news were full of friendly notices of Negro enterprises. Increasingly critical of capitalism, DuBois was always more of a race-conscious Negro nationalist than was Washington. By the 1930s, the depression conditions, his discouragement about the results of his lifetime struggle for integration, and his latent racial chauvinism caused DuBois, for a brief period, to advocate a separate Negro co-operative economy and separate schools. He justified these proposals, just as Washington had done two decades earlier, as tactics in the struggle for Negro integration into American society, but he later changed his mind. As we would hesitate to apply the term "accommodationist" to DuBois for this aberration, so, perhaps, we should be slow also to apply the term to Washington for his promotion of Negro segregated business.

We have seen that, in their economic thought, Washington and DuBois, at the turn of the century, were not far apart, and that Washington thought that, by promoting Negro business, he was putting his race's evolution in harmony with the economic revolution of his day. Washington's own life had shown that it was possible to be both a Negro and a successful, self-made American of the late nineteenth century. Along this line of reasoning, if not of action, he drew not only a handful of Negro businessmen and would-be businessmen, but most of DuBois's "Talented Tenth" of professional men whose interests were linked with his. This fisher of men caught many a lawyer, doctor, and teacher in his net, and their private correspondence is sprinkled with friendly references to the Business League. A *minority* of professional men—the group which Washington's friends called "the kickers" or "the soreheads"—

were opposed, not to promotion of Negro business, but
to its corollary: Washington's seeming lack of interest in
Negro political and civil rights, and his optimistic conviction—redolent of Samuel Armstrong and Adam Smith—
that every Negro's pursuit of his self-interest would, in the
long run, result in the race's interest. Even Washington's
opponents, though called "radicals," were not anticapital-
istic. Instead, they looked backward to an era when the
Negro professional class was dominant in the Negro community, hopeful of future integration into American society,
and favored by Northern philanthropy.

5. SETH M. SCHEINER

The Negro Church and the Northern City, 1890–1930

Richard Hofstadter has commented that "The United States was born in the country and has moved to the city." For no element of the population has this been quite so much a fact of life as for black Americans in the twentieth century. In 1890 more than 90 per cent of America's black population continued to be concentrated in the rural South. Three-quarters of a century later, only slightly more than half the black population remained in the South, and even within that section, blacks moved from the farm to the city. Today, Negroes are more urbanized than whites.

The first three decades of this century witnessed the beginnings of a significant shift in America's Negro population from the rural South to the urban centers of the North. Although historians and demographers have emphasized the enormous movement of Negroes to Northern cities during and following World War I, significant increases in Northern migration were recorded in the two decades preceding the war. A small number of blacks had made their way north between the end of the Civil War and 1890; but by 1910, black migration had doubled, and in some cases tripled, the black populations of Northern states. Nearly all those who migrated settled in urban areas. In 1920 New York and Philadelphia were the two cities in the nation with the largest Negro populations. Ten years later, one of every four Negroes had migrated from the South, and 90 per cent of Northern Negroes lived in urban *areas. Nearly a million black Americans lived in the nation's five major industrial centers: New York, Chicago, Philadelphia, Detroit, and Cleveland.*

This move from the environment of the rural South to the urban North put great strains on the institutions of the black community, strains intensified by both interracial and intraracial tensions. Although a number of books have been written on the development of Northern ghettos during these years, the ways in which the black community adapted to the urban environment institutional structures formed in the rural South have not been studied in any detail.

The well known report to the President by Daniel Patrick Moynihan opened a fruitful, if sometimes bitter, debate on family structure in the black community; but the adjustment of other major institutions remains unstudied. Certainly, this is true of the Negro church, which John Hope Franklin believes to be "the most powerful institution in the Negro's world. . . ." There can be little doubt that the number of churches proliferated as blacks migrated to the cities, and that the ministry has served as a constant source of leadership in the black community. The ability of some churches to marshal economic resources has played an important role in the development of Harlem and other black communities. Yet the growth of Marcus Garvey's quasi-religious Universal Negro Improvement Association, and later organizations such as the Black Muslims, indicates that the Negro church, as well as civil rights organizations such as the NAACP, did not meet all the needs of the alienated black masses in the urban environment.

Professor Seth Scheiner of Rutgers, the State University of New Jersey, focuses on the adjustment of the Negro church to the urban environment. Surveying the historical literature on this subject he concludes that the role of the church in the black community has been paradoxical. Black intellectuals in the 1920s and 1930s criticized the other-worldliness of the Negro church, and offered a number of explanations for the failure of the church to form a center for the organization of the black community in urban America. While accepting and emphasizing these criticisms, Professor Scheiner also points out that certain black churches and religious leaders have taken a leading role in racial protest. Thus, the themes of "accommodation" and "protest" which animate the entire history of the Negro in America are reflected in the experience of the Negro church in its attempts to adapt to the urban environment.

N EGRO settlement in Northern cities is not a recent phenomenon. Blacks have inhabited Northern cities for many years. For example, in New York City in 1820, Negroes formed 8.8 per cent of the population, though by 1860 the percentage was down to 1.5; in Philadelphia between 1820 and 1860, the Negro population ranged from 8.8 to 3.9 per cent. The reasons for this decline were the massive influx of European immigrants, especially in the 1840s and 1850s, and the limited actual growth of the Negro population. The Negro population in New York City, for example, went from 10,886 in 1820 to 12,581 in 1860. It was not until the 1890s, though, that Negro movement northward began to approach substantial proportions. Between 1890 and 1930 more than 2,500,000 Negroes left the South for the North. The migratory movements of this period were not limited to blacks; they were part of a national shift of population to the cities. In the course of the forty years between 1890 and 1930 the proportion of the nation's whites living in cities went from about 39 per cent to just under 58 per cent. For black Americans, the figure rose from 20 to 44 per cent.

Most blacks who moved northward settled in the cities. By 1930 almost nine of every ten Negroes living outside the South made their homes in urban centers, compared with only three out of five in 1890. Between 1900 and 1910 the Negro population of New York City rose by 51 per cent, that of Philadelphia and Chicago by 30 per cent. During the next ten years, 1910 to 1920, the black population increased by 59 per cent in Philadelphia, 66 per cent in New York, 148 per cent in Chicago, 308 per cent in Cleveland, and 611 per cent in Detroit. There was a downturn in Negro migration North in the early 1920s, but it picked up again around 1922, so that in the decade 1920–30 the black population in Philadelphia expanded by 64 per cent, in Chicago by 114 per cent, in New York by 115 per cent, in Cleveland by 109 per cent, and in Detroit by 194 per cent. Other Northern cities reported significant gains in their Negro population—Gary, Pittsburgh, Cincinnati, and Columbus (Ohio), to name a few.

A combination of propelling and attracting forces helps to explain the mass exodus of Negroes from the South to Northern cities. Economic deprivation, made even more difficult between 1914 and 1916 by a decline in wages, the ravaging effects of the boll weevil on the cotton crop, and the raging floods that drove many blacks from the land and their homes, provided the main push for blacks to leave the rural areas of the South for urban centers. Discrimination and mob violence were not the fundamental causes of Negroes' deserting the South; they served, instead, as re-enforcing factors. According to Louise P. Kennedy in her study *The Negro Peasant Turns Cityward,* those counties with the highest incidence of lynching reported an increase in their Negro population, whereas in areas in which the Negro population declined the white population did also. For the inequities of second-class citizenship to exert a significant push for blacks to leave their old homes, to follow Miss Kennedy's argument, there had to be a definite economic slump.

The North, on the other hand, seemed to offer the hard-hit Southern black a chance to escape his predicament. As a result of the drop in the number of European immigrants arriving in the United States after the outbreak of World War I—from 1,200,000 in 1914 to only 326,000 in 1915, 298,000 in 1916, and 110,000 in 1918—Northern industry had to look elsewhere for its labor supply. At first agents were sent South to recruit workers for Northern factories; but once the move North had begun, labor recruiters were no longer needed. Letters and visits from friends and stories in the Negro press of the opportunities in Northern cities proved sufficient to encourage more and more blacks to come North.

Scholars have examined how participants in a mass migration adapted to their new environment. For the Negro, studies have explored the relationship between urbanization and the family, the church, economic and housing conditions, cultural developments, and black nationalism. This essay will attempt an examination of how one institution of the Negro community—the church —adapted to life in the twentieth-century Northern city. It will explore the effects on the role played by the Negro church of the massive migration of blacks to Northern cities between 1890 and 1930. It does not pretend to be definitive; rather, it seeks to offer suggestions, and possibly a framework for further thought and research. Since this volume seeks to reduce citations to a minimum, only a portion of the sources consulted, both primary and secondary, will be mentioned.

The Negro church came into being early in the history of the United States. E. Franklin Frazier, among others, has spoken of its dual origins: first, as an "invisible insti-

tution" on the Southern plantation; second, as a reaction
to discrimination in white churches. It was this latter practice which led many blacks in Northern urban centers to
organize their own houses of worship. For example, a group
of Philadelphia Negroes had attended a predominantly
white Methodist church without incident until November
1787. On a Sunday in that month, the church's leaders
attempted to seat the blacks in the rear of the gallery.
Refusing to abide by this practice, the blacks, led by Richard Allen and Absalom Jones, left the church and organized the Free African Society. Before long Jones and Allen
went their separate ways. Jones established the first independent Northern Negro church, St. Thomas Protestant
Episcopal Church of Philadelphia. Allen organized the
Bethel African Methodist Episcopal Church in Philadelphia, dedicated in 1794. Other Negro Methodists followed
Allen's example and organized A.M.E. churches in other
cities, and in 1816 they joined together in a national African Methodist Episcopal Church.

The independent Negro church movement extended beyond the Methodist church. Among the separate Negro
churches were: Abyssinian Baptist and St. Philip's Protestant Episcopal in New York City, African Baptist in Philadelphia, and African Congregational in New Haven. While
some blacks retained their membership in predominantly
white churches, a majority affiliated with Negro houses of
worship. "By 1830," according to Leon F. Litwack in
North of Slavery, "the Negro church movement reflected
much of the chaos and multiplicity of sects that prevailed
among the whites." In the years that followed, the number
of churches and their membership expanded. By 1916,
there were 6,633 African Methodist Episcopal Churches,
claiming nearly 550,000 members.

Historically, Negro churches, both Northern and Southern, urban and rural, have played an important role in the

life of blacks. Carter G. Woodson, in his *History of the Negro Church*, observed that the Negro church "had to be overworked" to compensate for the destructive effects slavery and discrimination had upon Negro institutional life. Arthur Huff Fauset believes that "the apparent over-emphasis by the American Negro in the religious sphere is related to the comparatively meager participation of Negroes in other institutional forms of American culture." * The important place occupied by the Negro church in Negro society led C. Eric Lincoln to remark in *The Black Muslims in America* that "until fairly recent times, the Negro's church was the most important organization standing between him and the unremitting pressures of our caste-oriented society." The church became a place to pray, to meet friends, to be free, even for a brief time, from the insults of a hostile society. The church became the focal point of Negro society. Accordingly, a great burden was placed upon the shoulders of the Negro preacher. His church had to tend to more than spiritual matters. It became a social center, a promoter of education and cultural activities, a dispenser of aid to the needy, a social stabilizer for the black community, a force for social control as well as, on occasion, social reform and protest. Many a business venture had its origin through the auspices of the church. Houses of worship also served as places of birth for many benevolent and cultural societies and as meeting places for fraternal organizations in their formative years.

In the course of the period 1890 to 1930, however, the church declined significantly as the focal point of Negro life because of secular alternatives and internal weaknesses that impaired its ability to grapple with the ramifications of the urbanization process. By 1930 it no longer dominated the Negro community as it had earlier, even though it remained the single most important institution. One fac-

* *Black Gods of the Metropolis* (1944).

tor that undermined the Negro church's almost unchallenged pre-eminence in Negro society was success in terms of numbers. With the increased Negro migration to Northern cities, churches seemed to spring up almost overnight. New York City in 1865 contained 13 Negro churches; by the 1920s there were about 200. Chicago Baptist and Methodist churches went from 58 to 122 in the brief span of the four years between 1916 and 1920. In a survey of five selected Northern cities between 1916 and 1926, the number of Negro Baptist churches rose by 151 per cent and African Methodist Episcopal churches by 85 per cent.

Obviously, a large part of this growth can be attributed to population increase, but the evidence shows that most Negro churches had a limited number of members on their rolls, even though studies differ as to the size of the average Negro congregation. An investigation conducted by the Greater New York Federation of Churches in 1930 disclosed that while one in four Negro churches in the city had an average membership in excess of 1,000, three of four averaged only 122 members. Benjamin Mays and Joseph Nicholson, who used a somewhat larger sample in their comprehensive examination *The Negro Church*, estimated an average membership in 1930 of 586. Despite the different figures in the two studies, the Mays and Nicholson volume contains data to support the authors' argument that average Negro church membership was rather low. In Cincinnati, where the black population was 10.6 per cent of the total population, Negro churches accounted for 32 per cent of all churches in the city. In Detroit 7.7 per cent of the population was black; Negro churches represented 24 per cent of all churches. In Philadelphia 11.3 per cent of the population was black, while Negro churches were 24 per cent of the total number. These figures lead one to conclude that either more Negroes than whites were members of churches or that Negroes tended to cluster in smaller congregations than whites. Support for the latter interpretation (which does not necessarily contradict the former) comes from the Census of Religious Bodies for 1936. That census reported that Negro urban churches averaged 219 members as opposed to 616 for white urban houses of worship.

Such a high proportion of churches in the black community restricted not only the membership possibilities for individual churches, but the financial resources a church could draw upon. Even if there had been fewer Negro churches, they would still have run into difficulty in gaining support from a population that had limited economic opportunities. Mays and Nicholson found that less than one-half of the membership of urban Negro churches provided financial support. This state of affairs led them to remark that "the Negro is overchurched primarily because the available church money is so thinly spread over so wide an area . . . ."

The storefront or resident-type church accounts, in large part, for the proliferation of Negro churches in the cities between 1890 and 1930. Opening a storefront eliminated the time-consuming and costly process of erecting an edifice. If one rented a vacant store, he could start conducting services almost immediately. The storefront was also an outlet for the expression of leadership in a society that denied Negroes equal opportunity in many areas. Many a church was born as a result of a battle for leadership within an older house of worship, a phenomenon not, of course, limited to the period under examination. Studies of Negro religious life have noted how this struggle led to an even greater abundance of Negro churches. Against this background, storefront churches increased at a rapid rate as blacks streamed northward. In the mid-1920s storefronts comprised 39 per cent of the Negro churches in New York City; by 1930 observers placed three of every four churches in Harlem in this category. Mays and Nicholson's survey in 1930 of twelve Northern cities designated 37 per cent of the Negro churches as of the storefront variety. The proportion varied from city to city, but generally speaking it was high. Storefronts made up 45 per cent of the Negro churches in Detroit, 48 per cent in Philadelphia, and 72 per cent in Chicago.

While a large portion of the storefronts were of the revivalistic Baptist stripe (nearly half in the Mays and Nicholson volume), a substantial number followed the Holiness or Spiritualist cults.* Between 1928 and 1938 the number of Spiritualist houses of worship in Chicago went from seventeen to fifty-one (from one-twentieth of the total number of churches to one in ten). An examination of a number of Northern cities found that the Holiness and Spiritualist churches accounted for about 34 per cent of all Negro churches in those cities.

The storefront church performed an important function in attempting to facilitate the adjustment of the rural lower class to the urban North. The storefront provided a congenial environment to meet old friends or to make new ones among persons of similar background in the impersonal city. Its smaller membership made for warmer relations, a greater involvement in church affairs, and a sense of security not available in larger churches. Facing economic hardships, the crowded tenements, the rapid pace of urban life, and the unfamiliarity of the city, the lower-class migrant discovered in the storefront a piece of his rural past. These smaller houses of worship, like rural

---

* E. Franklin Frazier in *The Negro Church in America* describes the cults as follows: The Holiness cults "insist that Christians shall live free of sin and in a state of holiness. . . . By sin they mean the use of tobacco, the drinking of alcoholic beverages, cursing and swearing, dancing, playing cards, and adultery. . . . In recounting their achievement of a state of holiness, some members tell of having visions of heaven." The Spiritualist has some minor differences from the Holiness such as not being "opposed to card-playing, dancing, or 'sporting life.' "

churches and the larger urban churches, also compensated for the black man's exclusion from the mainstream of American society. They provided a place of insulation from the discriminatory practices of the wider community. For rural blacks "confronted for the first time with the problems of northern urban life," the storefronts, especially those groups that were not affiliated with the traditional denominations (such groups are commonly referred to as cults), served to relieve and release "psychological tensions." * In short, the storefront was "an attempt on the part of the migrants to re-establish a type of church in the urban environment to which they were accustomed." †

The widespread appeal of the storefronts, whether of the more traditional denominations or the cult groups, owed a great deal to the nature of their religious services. Through the fire and brimstone sermons, the exotic rituals, and the emphasis on a simple morality, newcomers could participate in a religion similar to that practiced in their former homes in the South. The storefronts provided a transition from the rural South to the urban North.

Critics have condemned the storefront church's otherworldliness as diverting its members from economic and social problems. This criticism is well taken, but it overlooks the fact that those of the lower class who see little hope of sharing in the material rewards of this world find solace in looking hopefully toward the spiritual rewards of the next. Charismatic preachers delivered sermons stressing a personal God who looked upon the masses as His favored people. Holiness churches, in particular, maintain that they are the descendants of the ordinary people Jesus lived among, thereby giving their lower-class members a sense of importance in a society that told them they were nothing. One commentator has attested to "the 'spiritual

---

* Fauset, *Black Gods.*
† Frazier, *The Negro Church in America.*

upward mobility' offered by the Holiness religion [that] serves as a psychological substitute for upward occupational and economic mobility." * In their otherworldly emphasis Negro churches and especially cult religions hold out to their members the promise of attaining justice in the next life.

While the storefronts in their own way attempted to re-create in the city a portion of the migrant's former home and served as a buffer against the vicissitudes of city life, their proliferation contributed to the fragmentation of the Negro church. No longer could the established churches present a united front in meeting the needs of the black community. Where a few churches might dominate the religious life of blacks in rural communities, small towns, or the early cities, in the twentieth-century city it was a different story. A host of churches battled with each other for adherents and influence. In *Black Chicago* Allan Spear tells how, before World War I, "the large, middle-class Baptist and Methodist churches had dominated Negro religious life," in contrast to the years that followed.

In both *Black Bourgeoisie* and *The Negro Church in America*, Frazier emphasizes the relationship between urbanization and increasing class stratification among blacks. Among Negro churches, even those of the same denomination, class division became more apparent as a city's black population increased. Lower-class blacks, on the one hand, found services at middle- and upper-class churches too restrained and the size of the congregations too large and forbidding. On the other hand, many of the middle- and upper-class churches attempted to divorce themselves from what they considered the overemotionalism of lower-class houses of worship. Through their places of worship, middle-class churchgoers often manifested their feelings of status

* Norvel Glenn, "Negro Religion and Negro Status in the United States," in Louis Schneider, ed., *Religion, Culture, and Society.*

and divorced themselves from the mass of blacks. Many an upward-striving Negro sought to attach himself to a more established Baptist church, or even an Episcopal or Presbyterian one.*

Class stratification in urban black communities was one factor hampering the Negro church from operating as a single unified force in the urban context. Although it may be possible for a small group to control and influence a large proportion of the population, this has not been the case in the black community. The fragmentation of the Negro church in urban centers between 1890 and 1930 impaired its attempts to play such a role. The plethora of churches restricted the activities of those houses of worship that sought to aid their more unfortunate compatriots. Church competed with church for influence, followers, and financial support.

Rivalry between churches was but one form of competition. As the period 1890–1930 progressed, secular agencies emerged to assume functions that the church had considered its province. Settlement houses, charitable organizations, and groups such as the Urban League, operated by white and blacks (in many cases predominantly by whites), increased in importance. Although some Negro ministers took part in the activities of these agencies, and the agencies cooperated with many Negro churches, the control, operation, and decision-making of the secular groups existed outside the framework of the Negro church. And as social work became more professionalized in the

---

* Note the comment of Frazier in *Black Bourgeoisie*: "As Negroes have moved up the social ladder within the Negro community, they have tended to desert the Baptist and Methodist churches and have affiliated with the Episcopal, Congregational, and Presbyterian churches." Certain comments here and elsewhere in this paper could also be applied to white Protestant churches; but the greater importance of the church in the Negro community has made for a more significant functional difference.

1920s—with the trained social worker replacing the volunteer—the church lost even more ground.

Fraternal societies and social clubs also were rivals of the church. Blacks found that these organizations, like the church, compensated for their exclusion from the wider community. During their formative years the fraternal and social groups used church buildings to hold their functions. As time passed, they took on an identity of their own and amassed financial resources. They relied less on houses of worship as places to meet, purchasing or renting facilities for their activities. These secular associations competed with churches for the time as well as the limited resources of Negro urbanites.

A competitor for the church that had an even wider appeal than the fraternal organizations and social clubs was public recreation. For the lower classes, who did not participate in organized social activity to the extent of other classes, public amusements were of particular value. A major portion of the recreational and cultural life that centered for so many years around the church shifted to the public arena. As the urban black community spread over a wider area and included more people, it offered a market for theaters, cabarets, sports events, and other forms of public amusements. In Harlem, for example, theaters lined such thoroughfares as Lenox Avenue. Thus, public entertainment provided an urban alternative to religion, and the church was no longer the all-pervasive institution it had been. In *Black Metropolis*, a study of Negro life in Chicago, St. Clair Drake and Horace Cayton found that the church received less coverage in the Negro press following the Great Migration than in earlier years. This and other evidence led them to conclude that the house of God was no longer "the center of community life" it had been before World War I. The urban black had other options.

Consequently, as Spear has argued in the case of Chicago, the Negro community "could no longer rely upon the institutions [the church and fraternal organization] that had dominated the civic life of rural and small town Negro communities. It now confronted urban problems that demanded urban solutions." *

By reacting to the transitions taking place in urban society with the simplistic morality of a past era, the clergy further undermined the authority of the Negro church. Ministers frequently condemned in highly moralistic tones the spread of secular entertainment in the city. Dancing, for example, was damned as heathen and demoralizing. Many clergymen referred constantly to a growing preoccupation with frivolous social events. By condemning in puritanical terms the social diversions that attracted more and more urbanites, both white and black, the church weakened its voice as a social force within the Negro community.

Critics have argued that the unwillingness or inability of many clergymen to recognize the appeal secular entertainment held for the masses was a manifestation of their otherworldly orientation. They have accused the church of being preoccupied with trivialities or the erection of ostentatious structures. In the early 1900s a New York Negro newspaper maintained that churches drained both "the time and small money of their membership." It asserted that the church leadership regarded "church building and money raising as the principal business of a preacher," and the good of a community as only secondary. James Weldon Johnson as early as 1915 charged that "a gross mercenary spirit permeated" the church. "And for what purpose is the money gathered?" The "great bulk of it," he concluded, "goes to maintain costly temples." And *The Crisis*, the organ of the NAACP, called upon the church to spend less time "inveighing against dancing and theater going"

* *Black Chicago.*

and more in positive programs of education and social uplift. In 1930 these assertions gained support from the work of Mays and Nicholson mentioned earlier. They found that in urban centers approximately 72 per cent of church budgets went for salaries, interest and the reduction of the church debt, and repairs. Johnson's impressionistic observations presaged the more scientific investigation of Mays and Nicholson. Some ten years before the latter study, Johnson bemoaned the "superfluous churches" that drained the financial resources of the community from more worthwhile ventures. Negro churches used more of their income for church building than for community action.

If the charge is valid that most Negro churches failed to meet the practical needs of the black masses, it is traceable to more than the proliferation of houses of worship, limited financial resources, and the assumption by secular agencies of functions formerly exercised by the church. The limited training of most ministers and their otherworldly orientation must share responsibility. C. Luther Fry's *The United States Looks at Its Churches*, based on the 1926 Census for Religious Bodies, estimates that 80 per cent of white urban Protestant clergymen had a college or seminary education, compared with only 38 per cent for blacks. In rural areas the proportion was lower for both whites and blacks—47 per cent for whites and 17 per cent for blacks. Mays and Nicholson, from their examination of a select group of Negro ministers, came up with an even lower figure. According to their study, about 28 per cent of the Negro urban clergy had graduated from a college or seminary. One reason for this low percentage of formally educated Negro clergymen is that many sects required only a calling to assume the pulpit, but white Protestants and white society in general must carry an even more substantial burden for this statistic. Whites denied blacks equal access to formal training on all educational levels. Far too

many colleges and seminaries, at least before 1930, discriminated against Negro applicants. Even though a larger
number of Negro ministers received formal training in the
first three decades of the twentieth century than in earlier
years, they remained a relatively small group. And the cloth
was declining in its appeal for the young. Many scholars
have attributed this development to a variety of factors,
including a wider range of opportunities for Negroes to
enter the professions in Northern cities, though still not
on a level with whites.

Cut off from equal educational opportunities at all levels,
most Negro clergymen were not privy to theological debates
and interdenominational cooperation. David Reimers as-
serts in *White Protestantism and the Negro* that the Social
Gospel movement of the late nineteenth and early twentieth centuries "scarcely considered" the Negro. Most
Negro churches and ministers were outside the Social
Gospel wing. Negro churches, especially the evangelicals,
according to William G. McLoughlin, writing in *Daedalus*
in 1967, moved outside the "context of the theological . . .
trends of the times." Already "racially alienated, they [the
Negroes] now became theologically alienated." *

The theological positions taken by the majority of Negro
ministers tended to be quite traditional. Their sermons were
frequently preoccupied with fire and brimstone. Mays and
Nicholson reported in 1930 that only one in four sermons
in urban Negro churches "touched on practical problems."
The majority of sermons stressed a simple morality and
were preoccupied with the next world. Ministers frequently
told their congregations that "God in his good time changes
things in this world. If not, in the next world His suffering
servants will be free of the trials and tribulations which
beset them on the earth." This lack of faith in obtaining

* He applies the same argument, "to a lesser extent," to Southern
white evangelicals.

justice in this world led many clergymen to project hope "to heaven above." Their sermons and services provided an emotional outlet for the frustrated masses but did not serve as a vehicle for meeting the realities of day-to-day life.

Most clergymen, it has been argued, avoided the issues of the day. "Ministers with their otherworldly interest," wrote August Meier in *Negro Thought in America*, "quite easily fell into an accommodating position." Similarly, Gunnar Myrdal, in his classic study *An American Dilemma*, charged the church with following a conservative path on practical problems by virtue of its concern with the hereafter. It acquiesced in the inequities blacks faced in a country that treated them as second-class citizens. And E. U. Essien-Udom in *Black Nationalism* has accused the Negro church of avoiding "the problems of the degradation of its people." Instead, it has fostered "indulgence in religious sentimentality," and has riveted "the attention of the masses on the bounties of a hereafter." In so doing, it has remained "a refuge, an escape from the cruel realities of the here and now."

To mention only the otherworldly side of the Negro church and to emphasize its failure to respond to black needs in the urban context is to give but part of the picture. Recent scholars have emphasized what Gary Marx, in his analysis of the relationship between religious attitudes and militancy among Negroes, in the 1967 *American Sociological Review*, called the "dual role of religion" as a defender of the status quo and as "a strong positive" force "in the movement for radical social change."

One of the earliest examples of the ambivalence of Negro religion is the nature of the independent Negro church's birth. "The establishment of the separate Negro church," Meier and Rudwick have written in *From Plantation to Ghetto*, "was both a form of protest against American racism and yet an accommodation to it." Absalom Jones and Richard Allen, as noted earlier, reacted to the anti-Negro attitudes of a predominantly white church by forming their own house of worship. Vincent Harding at a recent meeting of the Organization of American Historians went even further when he directed our attention to incidents of antislavery activity centered in the Negro church, and stressed "the ambiguity, the doubleness, of black religious experience" under slavery. Others have revealed the continuing activity of many of the black clergy. A substantial segment of black abolitionist agitation was either initiated by Negro preachers or revolved around their houses of worship. During Reconstruction, a large number of those blacks who assumed leadership positions in Southern states were ministers. Meier and Rudwick have also shown, in the 1969 *Journal of American History*, the role played by clergymen in the boycotts directed against Jim Crow streetcars early in this century, and they concluded that "the relationship of religion to Negro protest has always been paradoxical." *

It is also maintained that those sermons that do not deal specifically with day-to-day problems cannot be dismissed as mere palliatives. Many of the otherworldly sermons have used texts drawn from the Bible that show God's wrath for injustice and His favor for the equality of man. During the ante-bellum period clergymen frequently used the Scriptures to campaign against slavery. Miles Fisher in *Negro Slave Songs in the United States* has shown the presence in many spirituals of themes stressing resistance to the slave system. Even Benjamin Mays, an outspoken critic of the otherworldly emphasis of most sermons, ac-

---

* In his *Negro Thought*, Meier noted the paradox when he wrote that while most of the clergy took an accommodating position—one that he believes has been dominant—their "gradualist philosophy of self-help" included an appeal to "racial solidarity." As Meier points out, however, racial solidarity can be a form of accommodation to the existing system.

knowledges a "second trend" which presents God as standing for justice and equality.*

To a certain degree, black nationalist religious groups reflect the dichotomy between otherworldliness and protest in Negro religion. They, too, have "roots in . . . urban tensions and in the hopeless frustration which the Negroes experience in trying to identify themselves and their aspirations with white society." † But unlike most cults, the black nationalists are outspoken critics of the anti-Negro nature of American society. They are advocates of rectifying this situation in this life rather than putting it off to the next; they seek to overcome the "powerlessness" the lower class has experienced. The faith of such groups as the Black Muslims has been placed in a Supreme Being who will bring down His wrath upon white society and will reward blacks with freedom from white oppression on this earth. Black Muslim rhetoric is that of protest, not acquiescence; but for the Muslims the timing of redemption is in the hands of Allah.

Marcus Garvey's back-to-Africa movement of the 1920s, which contained a strong religious element, was another black nationalist organization that appealed to a redemptive God. "God will answer our prayers against the wicked and unjust," predicted Garvey, "and strengthen us for the great work that must be done in His name and to His glory." And like other black nationalists, Garvey spoke of a black God. Through the use of religious symbols colored black, Garvey sought to enhance self-pride among his fellow blacks. But Garvey differed from the Black Muslims in that he called for immediate steps to bring about a just society. Unlike the strictly otherworldly religious groups, Benjamin Mays maintains, Garvey used God "to stimulate the Negro to work to improve his social and economic

* *The Negro's God as Reflected in His Literature.*
† Essien-Udom, *Black Nationalism.*

conditions." If Garvey was mystical and unpractical in his call for a return to Africa, as some have charged, he did not urge indifference to the racist practices that permeated America.

It appears, then, that black nationalist religious groups, generally speaking, have assumed a posture of protest against the prevailing order while remaining apolitical. These religious groups, cults, and most churches with an otherworldly orientation have rejected political involvement. As for those appeals to the next world that lack the militancy of the black nationalists, while they tend to distract blacks from their everyday problems, they do contain elements of protest even if it is directed toward the hereafter. Yet, the compensatory strand undermines the church's ability to work as a force for change in the here and now. Possibly its relation to protest is in terms of a common theme that binds blacks together.

The ambivalence in Negro religion is also apparent in social action and politics. A number of clergymen participated in social reform and politics between 1890 and 1930. Reverdy Ransom, a minister of the African Methodist Episcopal Church involved in various reform ventures, established in 1900 the Institutional Church and Social Settlement in Chicago. Among its services were a day nursery, kindergarten, employment agency, and athletic facilities. St. Philip's Protestant Episcopal Church in New York City provided the black community with social services similar to those of the Institutional Church. Its pastor throughout most of the period under examination, Hutchens C. Bishop, worked with both the Urban League and the National Association for the Advancement of Colored People. Some ministers extended their interests into politics, usually in alliance with the political machine, a reform group, or a protest organization. Clergymen who participated in politics were not unanimous in their approach or

views. Certain preachers used the political arena to call
for equal treatment of blacks, while others accommodated
to the prevailing order. In politics as in social welfare,
though, the clergy's position was being pre-empted by persons or groups outside the church. Lawyers and businessmen moved into the Negro political vanguard and pushed
more and more clergymen into the background. Negro
newspapers also played a significant role in local politics,
and many of them were among the chief critics of the
church's involvement in politics. The conflict between press
and clergy may have reflected a struggle for influence in
the ghetto. Preachers also had to deal with challenges from
protest organizations such as the NAACP. Protest groups
presented still another alternative to the church even though
they varied in their degress of militancy.

There is need for further examination of the clergy's
participation in politics. Was its major posture protest or
accommodation? What factors account for a high or low
degree of militancy? Through what medium (the church,
the political party, or the protest organization) did those
ministers who engaged in politics operate? Was it increasingly necessary for such preachers to go outside the church
to be effective in politics or protest? What reception did
these men receive in the urban black community? From
what denominations and class level did the clerical activists
come?

Scholars have not fully investigated these questions, but
suggestions as to the relationship between political activism
and denominational affiliation are offered in a few works.
August Meier argues in *Negro Thought in America* that
the "more elite Presbyterian, Congregational, and Episcopal churches of the Northern and border states" were the
centers of protest thought between 1880 and 1915, while
the Baptist and Methodist churches with mass support
tended to be more conservatively inclined. James Q. Wil-

son's study of Chicago politics in the 1950s, *Negro Politics*, similarly shows that while the majority of Chicago blacks affiliated with churches were Baptists, most Negro civic leaders reported membership in such upper-class churches as the Episcopal, Presbyterian, and Congregational. It is noteworthy that while the elite Chicago churches could count only 10 per cent of the city's Negro citizens as their followers, the majority of Negro lay civic leaders came from these denominations. Additional support for the claim that greater activism exists in the more elite churches comes from the study by Gary Marx mentioned earlier. His survey, conducted in 1964, found greater militancy among Negro members of the Episcopal, Presbyterian, United Church of Christ, and Catholic faiths than among those of the Methodist, Baptist, and the multitude of cult churches. In fact, the least militant in Marx's investigation were members of sects and cults who have long been believed to be apolitical.

Marx's article contains a number of interesting hypotheses regarding the relationship between religious inclination and protest thought which may be relevant to other periods of Negro history. The persons he interviewed with an otherworldly orientation were less likely to advocate or support protest activities. But when Marx made a distinction between the "otherworldly" and the "temporal" among the religious in his sample, he found a relationship between religious feeling and militancy. For many of the temporal group religion seemed "to facilitate or at least not to inhibit protest." They drew upon the "universal humanistic values" that Marx sees playing "a strong positive role in the movement for radical social change." In short, a propensity toward a protest viewpoint "depends on the type of religiosity involved."

The Negro church may have served less as a force for social reform and protest than the noninstitutional folk religion of blacks that Joseph Washington speaks of in his

Black Religion. Washington advances the interesting thesis that the folk or black religion of Negro Americans "transcends all religious and socio-economic barriers which separate Negroes from Negroes." It is a "racial bond" that emerged from years of seeking escape from discrimination in American life for the "ultimate goals of freedom and equality by means of protest and action." The independent Negro church, according to Washington, has too often strayed from this theme. The folk religion he describes bears some resemblance to the humanistic outlook Marx spoke of in his essay.

As an institution, however, the Negro church declined as a vital force for change in the Northern city. It became fragmented. As the black population in cities increased and city life became more complex between 1890 and 1930, Negro churches could no longer command the following or influence they held in rural areas, small towns, or the early cities. There were too many churches that lacked a higher organizational structure to bind them together. The Negro church's internal weaknesses, reflected in the prevalence of an untrained clergy and a theology ill-suited to the vicissitudes of urban life, became evident in Northern cities. And the limited resources of a population that was not given equal opportunity made it difficult for individual churches to meet much more than the emotional needs of their adherents.

The great tragedy of the Negro church was that while its influence declined substantially in the period 1890 to 1930, it still remained in 1930 the single most important institution in the black community. White society had so circumscribed Negro life that the Negro church had to assume functions that in the white world were the responsibility of other institutions. As Mays and Nicholson in the early 1930s remarked rather poignantly: "It is not too much to say that if the Negro had experienced a wider range of freedom in the emotional and economic spheres there would have been fewer Negroes called to preach and fewer Negro churches."

It may be reasonable to conclude that Negro religion has been a vital force for change when it has resorted to the temporal tradition of those blacks who resisted discrimination as well as those who went beyond the otherworldly and institutional shortcomings of the church. Only when there is a "withering of Negro religiosity," Joseph Washington claims in somewhat exaggerated fashion, will blacks achieve true equality. "The first step in this direction is for him [the Negro] to disentangle his authentic black religion from the pseudo-religion to which Negro institutions and congregations pledge allegiance." Marx maintains that religious involvement can lead only to "widespread radicalization of the Negro public" when its main concern becomes the problems of blacks on this earth and it accepts the principle that man and God can solve these problems in this lifetime. But he reminds us of the dualism of Negro religion: "Many militant people are nevertheless religious." Here, then, is the paradox in Negro religion—conflicting strands of protest and accommodation. Further research may bring more light to this paradox by focusing upon the relationship between beliefs, institutions, and the types of protest or accommodation pursued.

6. JAMES F. BARNES

Carl Stokes: Crisis, Challenge, and Dilemma

*The depression of the 1930s slowed the northward migra-
tion, but the economic opportunities associated with war
production drew blacks north in increasing numbers during the following decades. By 1960, more than three million Negroes (17 per cent of the total black population)
lived in the five major industrial cities of the North, and
another 900,000 had moved to the two major population
centers on the West Coast. At the same time, blacks within
the South had become increasingly urbanized and one-third
of all American Negroes lived in Southern cities.*

*This mass migration from the rural South, accompanied
by the flight of whites to the suburbs, resulted in concen-
trations of Negroes in sufficient numbers in many urban
areas to make them a politically viable force. In Chicago,
Detroit, and Cleveland, as well as in Atlanta and Dallas,
blacks have had, for many years, sufficient numbers to
hold the balance of power, but they have been unable to
translate this into effective political control. Although Detroit has two Negro Congressmen, nonpartisanship and a
general ticket in local elections kept the Common Council
"lily white" until 1957. Today there are indications that
urban blacks are becoming politicalized, and the recent
victories of Richard Hatcher and Carl Stokes, along with
the increasing number of black city councilmen and state
legislators, indicate that the situation may be changing.*

*Certainly the growing political power of blacks, the ele-
vation of members of the race to Congress, their appoint-*

*ment to the Cabinet and to the Supreme Court as well as
to positions of local power, offer hope for the future. Yet,
since the early fifties, the relative positions of whites and
blacks have diverged in crucial areas of employment, income, and education. Like most whites at an earlier date,
blacks left their farms for the city in search of economic
opportunity and a better life. Too often their dream of
the "promised land" has been betrayed. In place of the
legal segregation in the South was the de facto segregation
in the North. The urban ghetto, with its family disorgani-
zation, substandard housing, unemployment and under-
employment, and inferior schools has become the environment shaping the Negro experience in the mid-twentieth
century.*

*Although the plight of the black ghetto-dweller can be
traced, to a limited extent, to his lack of effective political
power, it is clear that the election of more black
mayors and city council members will not, in itself, solve all
these problems. In the following essay, Professor James
Barnes of Ohio University cautions us against the easy
assumption that the election of black mayors, even of the
quality of Carl Stokes, will provide the solution to our
urban problems. The problems of the cities, he argues,
while encompassing the question of race, transcend it. To
deal effectively with these problems, Americans will have
to reject what one historian calls the "American secular
culture of privatism," with "its concentration upon the individual and the individual's search for wealth," in favor
of normative behavior more in line with the social neces-
sities created by the urban environment.*

INTEREST in urban politics generally, and black politicians
and politics specifically, is quite clearly a result of the "long
hot summers" of recent years. For many persons, however,

interest in things black is a novelty, and interest in the politics and politicians of black communities too often represents simply a dishonest desire to "keep it cool" and avoid the reality of misery and exploitation that characterizes the life of millions of ghetto residents. As many Americans continue to be more impressed by the need for "law and order" than by a need for extensive social change, they will wait in vain for Carl Stokes or Richard Hatcher or Washington's Walter Washington to perform a series of miracles.

It is important to assess Carl Stokes's victory in Cleveland. As Cleveland's first black mayor, Stokes is certainly an indication of things to come, whether perceived as a conscious dimension of Black Power, or simply as a reflection of the changing demographic reality of the central cities. From either standpoint, Stokes's election signals an overdue infusion of action and energy into Cleveland's city government and administration. If one compares Stokes with his immediate predecessor—the rather unexciting Ralph Locher—Stokes brings to the position a potential for leadership demanded by the nature of our urban centers. This analysis is not designed to rekindle a spark of faith in the American dream, except in the sense that revivals and faith may be meaningful components of social change provided they do not become merely emotional catharses that reinforce political inaction.

I

Students of government are quite familiar with the concept of "caretaker government," an often imprecise, yet significant, set of attitudes about the proper responsibilities of government. A fundamentally conservative view of government, the caretaker concept is similar in tone and substance to the familiar nineteenth-century economic concept of *laissez faire*. The values represented stress the roles of private actors, assigning to the economic realm major responsibilities in the supply of capital and income distribution. A government can always, if it so desires, affect income distribution or capital supply by consciously manipulating its power of taxation. A minimal use of this power is likely to represent either an assessment of political realities or an ideological position, or both. The guidelines of caretaker government minimize the extent to which government participates in an arena perceived as one reserved for private decisions. Thus, personal savings and individual frugality are of greater value than public assistance programs. Unemployment and welfare programs receive grudging support from an administration that objects fundamentally to expenditures of public funds and values more highly the intervention of private enterprise or private charity. Government is expected to provide a minimal level of traditional municipal services. Experimentation and innovation are values assigned to the economic world; government is the proverbial necessary evil.

What is most critical to note, given the consequences for political activity, is the extent to which the dynamics of urban life generate extensive pressures for innovation and creativity. As suggested, however, the value pattern underlying caretaker government does not correspond to any conception of an imaginative, creative city hall leadership expending large sums of money for welfare programs, ghetto education, and so on.

The crisis in urban America is not simply a question of solving certain specific problems such as finding jobs or building houses. The crisis has an important intellectual dimension. We are being called upon to assess the basis upon which the urban environment will challenge the future. We have not yet achieved a set of political values that provides the basis from which many individuals are able to perceive the necessity for change or are guided in their efforts to effect change.

We must now evaluate established assumptions in response to the realities of a centralized mass society. We require a fresh intellectual perspective that will allow the formulation of new myths for new realities. It is our avoidance, or at best, our nonrecognition of the relevance of theoretical formulations about the urban environment that may sustain our inability, or rationalize our unwillingness, to treat humanely and effectively our many problems.

The most serious of these problems is the relationship of black and white in a society that abhors violence yet continues to give it a sacrosanct role in its mythology. We must do far more than recognize the existence of prejudice and hatred. We must achieve a perspective about our environment that allows isolation and analysis of those dimensions of life that exacerbate racial hostility, at the same time seeking to persuade men of the beauty and meaningfulness of the concept of human equality. I am not, naively or bitterly, asking for the time-worn appeal to the equality of man but asking how government as a community institution might have an impact on the resolution of our many social problems. If we are to confront the urban crisis with seriousness and sophistication, we must first recognize what it is, and what we, as a society, are about.

Interest in urban affairs leads naturally to a broad concern about man's relationship to man and his relationship to his environment—leisure, job, family, church, and educational system. Our failure to resolve the urban crisis should not, at some future time, be explained glibly by historians as our failure to accept the ideas of brotherhood and equality, but as our failure to use our ingenuity to minimize the private fears and frustrations of individuals. The significance of such persons as George Wallace or Louise Day Hicks is their politicizing of a not insignificant number of persons who view the world around them with fear, suspicion, and hostility. We have created those fears by our glorification of the virtues of material things, and by our callousness and immorality in supporting political candidates who seek to manipulate those fears. It is the task of our political and educational institutions to accept the challenge of education and not cater to ignorance and bigotry as a means of achieving consensus. Our stress on consensus has served only to depreciate the value of social criticism and legitimize personal aggrandizement and collective greed.

These prefatory comments about urban life in general reflect a strong belief on my part that political analysts do us a great disservice when they exclude the normative or ethical dimension of politics. I have tried to set forth a generalized series of concerns which I hope will serve as a broad backdrop for our interest in black politicians.

II

Cleveland, Ohio, is similar to any number of America's population centers. It has all the common urban illnesses —blight, air and water pollution, slums, and racial tension. The white exodus to suburbia is as characteristic of Cleveland as it is of Detroit, St. Louis, or Washington, D.C. Cleveland is experiencing every pain associated with urbanization in this country. The conservative values of caretaker government have shaped Cleveland's reaction to these problems. The old regime was unequaled in its dull responses to the challenges—challenges similar to those existing in every major American city. As is quite often the case in American politics, local governments respond favorably to the signals and direction of prestigious economic interests such as banks, newspapers, and chambers of commerce. Their views on such critical subjects as taxation may only rationalize the natural inclinations of public officials to oppose new taxation schemes or to authorize extensive public expenditures. It is our continuing attraction to the "rugged individual" and to the myths of frontier life that has produced so often the public and private myopia that characterizes our answers to many problems. Our refusal, for example, to distinguish "handouts" from legitimate public assistance is an indication of this malaise. Until there is broad acceptance of the idea of social responsibility and an awareness of the constraints on individual initiative, our public and private responses will continue to result in futility and despair. We must, at some point, accept the idea that man's interdependence is the hallmark of urban society. The mythology of frontier independence and aggressiveness should be relegated to the trashbin.

In his effort to become mayor of Cleveland, Carl Stokes had two significant advantages over his opponent in the Democratic Party primary, the incumbent mayor Ralph Locher. First, criticism about conditions in Cleveland had become commonplace. Lake Erie and the Cuyahoga River support little but jokes about the dangers of fishing, swimming, and the area's water supply. Cleveland's port facilities required long overdue expansion; the federal government, charging maladministration, had frozen the city's urban renewal funds; and the Hough area riot of 1966 had focused belated attention on the stark realities of ghetto existence. In sum, Cleveland and Ralph Locher were being called to account for decades of immobility. Locher, like his recent predecessors, reigned but did not rule. There is little evidence to counter the argument that Locher's view of his role was that political officials should function to facilitate the goals of economic interests. Locher's subservience was not, however, simply an expression of his gratitude for political support, but a manifestation of a broadly accepted value about the secondary role of government in the community. Locher's lack of response to the growing intensity of Cleveland's problems was predictable. An adherent of the caretaker approach receives no assistance from this negatively oriented concept in such circumstances. A myriad of problems associated with urbanization and industrialization filter through this conceptual apparatus as "crime in the streets" and lack of "law and order." Our seemingly inherent passion for individualism is incredible.

Carl Stokes also had an obvious advantage with the black community, an advantage one might be tempted to overemphasize, but an advantage nevertheless. Cleveland's black community is approximately one-third of the city's 900,000 residents, and represents well over 90 per cent of the black population of the Cleveland metropolitan area.

As might be expected, this black population is not distributed at random throughout the city. Of Cleveland's black citizens, 99.5 per cent live east of the Cuyahoga River, the city's east-west demarcation line. The point to note is the "natural" division of the city into two physically separate communities.

It is quite apparent that no aspirant for the mayoralty could rely simply on the black one-third for victory. And the black vote is, to some degree, a fiction of stereotyped imaginations. Like the well-known "labor vote," it must be cultivated and mobilized. Given the heterogeneity of the black community, no candidate for office, even a black candidate, can assume support.

Stokes's advantage was not simply his blackness; in fact, several observers have pointed out that many black citizens were indeed suspicious of his blackness. In a society that has created "Uncle Toms," any black politico must bear the judgment of his peers that he is being used by that society to further its goals and not those of the black community. Stokes's advantage was an established political relationship with the black community and assistance from key individuals and organizations within the community. His decision to seek the mayoralty was not his first effort to achieve public office. A graduate of the Cleveland–Marshall Law School, Stokes was an investigator for the State Liquor Control Board, an assistant city prosecutor, and, in 1962, the first black Democrat elected to the Ohio General Assembly. In an Assembly predominantly white and rural, Stokes's presence alone was a source of publicity. His decision to challenge Locher was not that of a novice to the local or state political scene.

The key to victory was strong black support and—critically—support from the white community. At this point a note of caution: We forget easily that descriptions of communities as black or white may tell us little about their political behavior. Except from the vantage point or perspective of the black community, the idea of a white community is a meaningless *political* concept. There is little justification for a white voter to support a white candidate on the basis of pigmentation. For the black community, however, a basis of power founded on a community of black interests is a necessary condition for social change. That many white voters have perceived the black man's thrust for equality as a threat is a devastating comment on the fragile foundations of security in this society. Thus, Cleveland's white community might be expected to respond as hostile whites, or as Republicans, or as liberals, or as Democrats. The often nonexistent, but journalistically predicted, "white backlash" is rooted in the lack of appreciation for the intensity of such political allegiances.

It is to this heterogeneous community that the records of Cleveland administrations of the past decade became important. The fears of some white voters about the possibility of a black mayor were minimized as discussion of Cleveland's problems and difficulties was emphasized. In sum, Stokes's strength in the black community and an important basis of support among liberal voters on the heterogeneous West Side provided a narrow margin of victory in the party primary. It was this same basic coalition that defeated Republican Seth Taft, of Ohio's famous Republican Taft family, in the November general election.

Seth Taft had certain disadvantages in this contest. For one thing he was not a "true" Clevelander but an expatriate suburbanite from exotic Pepper Pike. In a very interesting way, Taft and Stokes reflect the development of America's metropolitan areas. Tafts and would-be Tafts are the founders and inhabitants of suburbia, while the city remains the domain of the black man and other nationality groups, for whom the "melting pot" is a useless kitchen utensil.

Stokes defeated Taft by 2,000 votes. Stokes did quite well in the East Side wards—winning more than 90 per cent of the votes cast—while receiving approximately 20 per cent of the white West Side vote (final count: 129,000 to 127,000). Stokes did what every observer knew was essential: He was able to withstand predictable centrifugal forces within his major bloc of support, and to demonstrate to a significant number of white electors that he alone would be able to direct Cleveland's response to their common problems.

As is usually the case in politics, trouble begins upon election, since the view from the mayor's office varies significantly from the perspective of a candidate seeking that office. This is not to suggest that power corrupts, but to note the limitations inherent in political office. Neither should one forget the danger of harboring lofty expectations about change that are valid only in the minds of those who arrive at their Finland Stations. To effect change, one must overcome inertia, whether in the minds of Bolivian peasants or the lonely crowds of our urban centers. Stokes has encountered difficulty in reviving the dormant

concept of civic pride in Cleveland. His most exciting program—"Cleveland Now"—is an effort to enlist the financial aid of Clevelanders and the federal treasury in an
ambitious project of physical rehabilitation.

Stokes's ultimate challenge is the development of a community consciousness. This appears to be one motive of
"Cleveland Now." For, as I think Carl Stokes realizes, any
significant effort to alleviate present conditions will require the total commitment of each community in the
Cleveland area, reinforced by funds from the state and
federal treasuries.

A project like "Cleveland Now" can be viewed favorably
as a much-needed endeavor to engage community interest
and participation. It is also an admission of the anachro-
nistic nature of the local tax structure, particularly the
reluctance of Americans to look to the world of gigantic
corporate profits as a source of local revenue. The city's
change of complexion has been accompanied by drastic
changes in its revenue base. Although large corporate
bodies remain in many of our cities, their owners and per-
sonnel have, in most instances, become suburbanites, captured by the illusions of a station-wagon and swimming-pool
existence. Although willing to invest in an excellent sym-
phony orchestra, few Cleveland area suburbanites show any
interest in supporting the city's welfare or educational programs. The movement toward suburbia, and the physical
separation of Cleveland's black and white communities,
has served to fragment the resources and the talent available for a concerted attack on innumerable problems. It
is the insensitivity of suburbia, as well as the despair and
misery of our cities, which may indeed destroy us.

Carl Stokes will have to work hard to achieve re-election
in 1969. He is, necessarily, in this society, caught between
the rising aspirations and militancy of the black community
and the "law and order" hypocrisy of many whites. The

mood in Cleveland is described best as apprehensive. Of a number of political volcanoes to watch, the most volatile is the black ghetto—300,000 black citizens who remain, in varying degrees, victims of a system that simultaneously rewards and punishes them by granting and withholding the means to their personal and collective salvation. If one emulates Horatio Alger, the limitations and constraints on mobility become apparent; if one does not, contempt and repression are realities. This is the contradiction of America, a contradiction that has revitalized concepts of separatism and imbued many young blacks with a deadly fatalism.

III

Stokes's greatest test has taken place. Relationships between black communities and local police are strained everywhere in the United States and, in Cleveland, two critical events have transformed a strained relationship into a bitter feud. Although it is too early to determine the results, a brief discussion of these incidents will illuminate Stokes's dilemma.

The announcement of Martin Luther King's assassination was followed by a series of disturbances in Cleveland's Glenville area. In an effort to minimize the loss of life and general destruction, Mayor Stokes ordered the withdrawal of *all* white policemen from the immediate area. Stoke's decision was based on his judgment that the presence of white policemen would increase tension and possibly provoke serious confrontations between the police and many Glenville residents. The responsibility for restoring calm was delegated to the community itself. Various leaders of the community, in conjunction with the Mayor and members of his administration, labored to restore calm and ultimately were successful.

The reaction to this decision was hostility from many policemen, who felt that their professional integrity had been questioned, and great outcries from many others in Cleveland who felt that the black Mayor was being unduly soft on "black troublemakers."

The second event was a highly publicized encounter between a small group of black nationalists and white policemen, resulting in the death of several policemen. This encounter has been described both as an ambush undertaken by the black nationalists and as a trap devised by white policemen to "get" certain nationalist figures. The coverage of this event by local and national media created the specter of an armed black ghetto eager to assassinate all whites in northern Ohio.

My purpose in mentioning these two events is not to pass judgment on Stokes's decision, or to attempt to clarify the confusion surrounding the nationalist-police encounter, but simply to demonstrate the polarization of views that has taken place, and to analyze briefly the nature of this polarization. There is little doubt that such a process has been underway for some time. And by polarization, I do not mean physical separation—this has been a fact of life for years. What we are witnessing now is a polarization of goals and of thoughts on how best to achieve those goals. It is here that one finds the tragedy of American life and the fundamental source of our national dilemma.

Until recently, most black Americans have been staunch adherents of integration, and many continue to cling to this vision of society. It is, however, a vision that many have rejected, and many others have begun to doubt. Why has this happened? What has caused the dream to fade?

I think that the answer can be seen clearly in the refusal of millions of white Americans to perceive the reality that they must face and the contradictions between their everyday world and their world of mythology and illusion. One

is confronted constantly in this society with the incongrui-
ties of stated beliefs and empirical findings. Americans
continue to cherish the myths of the "market economy"
in an era of extensive corporate planning and control of
prices and quality. Americans continue to value the "self-
made man" in an era of industrial-military influence over
the course of the economy and national policy. We must
remember that in discussing the crisis of the cities, we are
discussing the crisis of society. The problems of the cities
must not be perceived as apart from, and unrelated to,
broader questions about political and economic relationships. Our cities *are* the society, despite the lingering notion
that somehow suburbia will shelter persons from the realities of life. It is when one contemplates the problem of
unemployment in the cities that one is aware of the future
of suburbia. If one responds, for example, to the problem
of unemployment by suggesting that jobs are the answer,
one is refusing to respond to the challenge of automation.
We have not yet abandoned our fascination with anachro-
nistic ideas about work and faced the greater challenge—
leisure time and its productive uses. Suburbia is predicated
on success; but a success rooted in a work ethic that is
increasingly threatened by the computer and the cybernetic
revolution.

Black Americans have been confronted for years by
economic and political realities that many white Americans
refuse to accept. Black Americans are drawing valid conclusions that many Americans find meaningless. It is in the
complex nature of this contradiction that one finds the
dilemma, a dilemma that is tragically simple and inherently
dangerous.

American society has created an oppressed, exploited
black America. And it has done so while reciting the Decla-
ration of Independence, the preamble to the Constitution,

and the resounding words of Lincoln's Gettysburg Address. It is the reality of this exploitation that millions of Americans resolutely refuse to accept. For them, the American dream appears to be a reality. I am convinced, however, that the frustration and anger of white America against black America is evidence of the inability of a society to live without a conscience or a set of values that provides psychic peace and comfort.

For many whites, blacks are troublemakers; and for most blacks, white society is the oppressor. The tragedy of America is that this society is intellectually unable to accept the reality of economic and political exploitation. If persons are poor, the reason must be, according to most whites, that they lack the desire to "change their station in life." Few among us are willing to discuss such phenomena as chronic unemployment, automation, and job discrimination. Welfare recipients are viewed as "shiftless," not as victims of a system that limits their skills and aspirations. I find much of the argument for individualism increasingly defensive. I hope that this means that the contradictions are now more apparent. As suburbia confronts drug addiction, school dropouts and delinquency, perhaps the hollowness of the dream will cause it to shatter. I recognize that this is a machiavellian point of view. For what I am arguing is that perhaps we must encounter misery in all our lives before we begin to recognize that misery exists.

It is from the comfort and convenience of such suburban mythology that one describes blacks as troublemakers and welfare recipients as shiftless. It is from this perspective that the charge of police brutality is perceived as the clever defense of "a criminal element" whose presence is a general threat. There will be police brutality, under whatever guise, as long as this society authorizes it. The answer that policemen require better salaries and working conditions avoids this latter point. The real answer lies in comprehending the economic and political facts of life. Unless there is substantial social change, blacks will continue to be trouble-makers, and if white America continues to operate within its bewildering world of contradictions, there will be police brutality. It is this hard reality that we must face. Many Americans are increasingly unable to live in their world wrapped in plastic and bombarded by propaganda against tooth decay; it is hardly incredible that they are unable to absorb the demands of the black population.

The ultimate tragedy of the black revolution is its blackness. For this revolution to succeed, there must be a corresponding revolution that allows America to resolve its contradictory existence. To conclude, as some have done, that the answer is black economic, political, and social separatism, *i.e.*, a black nation, is to ignore staggering technological realities. For better or worse, the future of America's black population is necessarily a function of the direction of the total society. I am not denying the need for black identity or black economic and political power. I simply find it difficult to envision a viable separation that would not, in fact, create a more dependent, more exploitative relationship than that existing in present circumstances.

The revolution must be one that creates a political-economic mythology compatible with urban living. Cities are the carriers of civilization; it will be Cleveland, and not Pepper Pike, that will be regarded as an index of quality in American life. That our cities are being destroyed is an indication that our society is fragile. Our national unwillingness to repair the damage is an indication that our technological genius is a genuine handicap to our capacity to resolve human misery.

IV

Carl Stokes exists in the midst of this complexity and confusion. Obviously, he cannot resolve the ills of Cleveland, as they are the ills of America. He can direct, assist in the general education of citizens, and seek a relationship among the various interests that best promotes the common good. But I am inclined to believe that our society is not willing to create the conditions for Stokes's success. He may be re-elected, and perhaps that is a healthy sign, but I doubt if we are willing to give to our public officials the power and resources required to direct a concerted effort. Our cities and our city officials are victims themselves, victims of a legal-political system that distrusts public power yet exalts the holder of private power as the benefactor of all mankind.

Stokes is creative, imaginative, and energetic. There are few politicians who warrant this praise. Yet these qualities are minimized by the ignorance of many apparently secure persons for whom any hint of change is seen as a serious threat. In this distressing fact is the dilemma of Cleveland. It is, quite clearly also, the dilemma of American society. Carl Stokes doesn't require our blessing. He needs our help.

7. CHARLES V. HAMILTON

Black Power: An Alternative

The Black Power movement which we are witnessing today represents the latest phase in the Negro revolution in this country, and no aspect of that revolution has been more difficult for whites to understand. This has been particularly true of the Negroes' former white allies in the civil rights movement who have been frustrated by black self-righteousness, by the tincture of antisemitism, and by the abusive disdain for "liberals" evinced by the Black Power spokesmen.

The Negro revolution has gone through a series of phases during the past three decades, each calling forth new tactics and new leadership. In its early stages the revolution was dominated by liberal whites and the Negro upper class and directed toward securing constitutional rights through continuous litigation and pressure. The very success of this action and its impact upon the Negro masses caused a shift in the center of support. Gradually the "Movement" came under Negro leadership and found support among the black working class. With this came a shift in tactics and goals. A greater emphasis was placed upon direct action to secure the elevation of the Negro masses. As the revolution evolved through law suits, bus boycotts, sit-ins, and freedom rides the role of whites in the "Movement" changed and new organizations and strategies emerged.

One of the new organizations to appear in the 1960s and the one originally responsible for the articulation of the demand for Black Power, was the Student Nonviolent

Coordinating Committee. SNCC grew out of the direct action movement begun with the bus boycotts in the middle fifties and the student sit-ins in the early sixties. It was characterized by the youth and militancy of its members— mostly young students and ex-students—and has been described as "more a spiritual community than a formal organization." Dedicated to transforming the society from the grass roots, the SNCC workers moved into Southern communities and lived on subsistence wages like the members of those communities.

SNCC began its activity with a voter registration drive in 1961 in McComb, Mississippi, which eventually led to the formation of the Mississippi Freedom Democratic Party, and until 1964 it was a biracial organization. The crucial events which shifted SNCC in the direction of Black Power occurred in that year. The "Mississippi Summer" project, which brought hundreds of young white students to the state to work in the black community, ended in tragedy, and revealed the many racial, class, and personal conflicts in the movement as it then existed. Secondly, the failure of the "liberal establishment" to support the MFDP at the Democratic Convention soured the young black radicals on coalition politics. At the same time the SNCC leadership, influenced by Malcolm X and the Algerian psychiatrist Frantz Fanon, moved toward a new emphasis on "blackness." Thus, during the march in June 1966, after the shooting of James Meredith, the stage was set for the appearance of the Black Power slogan.

Although Black Power immediately caught the imagination of Negroes throughout the country, its meaning was, and continues to be, somewhat ambiguous. In the essay that follows Charles V. Hamilton, the author (with Stokely Carmichael) of Black Power: The Politics of Liberation in America, *and Ford Professor of Political Science at Columbia University, presents a framework within which the*

Black Power movement can be understood and related to
the continuing process of political development. The es-
sence of Professor Hamilton's essay is that Black Power
represents a creative response to the mass pathology en-
gendered in the black community by years of oppression
and degradation. The analytical concepts he uses are drawn
from recent studies of the political response to the anomie
of mass society and the literature on the process of political
development of the emerging states of Africa and Asia.

Professor Hamilton sees Black Power as an alternative
not merely to other strategies for American blacks, but as
a crucial beginning of a modernization process in American
society. Perhaps Professor Hamilton is overly optimistic
about the possibilities of the Black Power movement, but
clearly the Negro revolution in our time is building a sense
of community among black Americans; and they are mov-
ing toward the creation of organizations relevant to their
peculiar situation. This cannot help having a decisive impact
on the future course of American development.

I WOULD like to suggest the thesis that the Black Power
movement is probably the most healthy, viable, and, indeed, the most significant political development in this
nation's history. In order to justify this claim, which may
at first seem extravagant, this essay will deal with three
major aspects of the phenomenon of Black Power. First,
I will discuss some concepts and theories essential to an
understanding of recent developments. Secondly, I shall
describe some specific programs and plans in pursuit of the
principle of Black Power. Finally, I should like to deal
briefly with the phenomenon of violence—social violence
—and its relation to Black Power.

Before I get into these topics, it is important to establish
that there are several different meanings of Black Power.

That this is so is understandable. These are dynamic times; emotions are high; change is rapid. The Black Power movement of the late 1960s is, indeed, a young movement. Although the term itself is not new (Marcus Garvey talked about Black Power in the 1920s, and in 1954 Richard Wright wrote a book about the new nation of Africa—Ghana—entitled *Black Power*), it has been projected into the racial struggle in this country in a pervasive way only since June 1966.

It is possible to identify at least seven distinct meanings of Black Power. To some people Black Power means racial pride; black consciousness; self-respect. This is the psychological component, with emphasis on black culture, history of black Americans, heritage, "soul." There is a second meaning: hatred of whites; kicking whites out of the civil rights movement. A third meaning is violence. Some people, when they hear the term "Black Power," immediately think of riots by black people, such as those that have occurred periodically since July 1964. Notions of "Burn, Baby, Burn" come to mind. A fourth meaning has been articulated by the new President, Mr. Nixon: black capitalism. This understanding of Black Power stresses the ownership of businesses by black people, with particular (though not exclusive) emphasis on small retail enterprises in the black community. A fifth meaning is separatism. Black Power means to some people (black and white) that black Americans should strive toward the goal of establishing a separate black nation. Usually the demand is that such territory should be carved out of certain existing states in the United States. There is not a strong movement among Black Power advocates to migrate to Africa as a separatist alternative. For others, Black Power is the epitomy of pluralist politics. These people understand Black Power to be in the oldest tradition of American pressure group politics; it is really no different from Irish Power, Jewish Power, or Italian

Power. This view concludes that, to a large extent, American politics is ethnically based and that black Americans should and must support members of their own race for political office in the same way that other groups support their own. The seventh, and final, meaning has to do with black community control. This conception of Black Power focuses on the necessity that black people control the institutions of decision-making in their communities whenever and however the situation permits: in education, law-enforcement, politics, economics, recreation, or community health.

All these meanings are related to Black Power, and it would be difficult, if not impossible, to reconcile some of them. In fact, at this moment, I suspect that such a reconciliation is not absolutely necessary. Different groups will act in their own way, depending on their styles, temperaments, and talents. And this is all part of the ferment and dynamism of the movement today. Thus, I shall proceed to elaborate on Black Power as *I* mean it and advocate it.

I

The following concepts are essential to understanding Black Power: alienation; relevant intermediary groups; and political modernization. It is important to understand these concepts before launching into a particular description of Black Power.

Alienation. Frequently, we hear that increasing numbers of black people are becoming alienated, especially the youth. A definition is in order. I suggest, in line with the definition put forth by Seymour M. Lipset, in *Political Man*, that when the social and political institutions no longer operate in line with the values and hopes of particular groups—as perceived by those groups—those institutions will be considered illegitimate, and the groups will become alienated from them. That is, the institutions will not be seen as functional. This does not mean that the institutions are "illegal"; indeed, they probably are legally constituted, but they are none-the-less *illegitimate*. They are no longer perceived as valid to the lives of some for whom they are supposed to be operating. Thus, in the past, it was not relevant that some decision-makers *said* that progress was being made in race relations. What was important was: What did the black masses *believe*?

In this connection, many people often forget what Stokely Carmichael and many of his colleagues were doing in the early years of the 1960s. They were working diligently and faithfully in the South on voter-registration and setting up Freedom Schools. Believing in the efficacy of the system, they filed hundreds of petitions to the United States Department of Justice complaining of harrassment by whites, beatings, and murders. Little was done to protect them. After a point, many of the young members of SNCC became alienated. They lost faith in the legitimacy of the institutions of decision-making. In a real sense, the political system failed *them*.

When groups and individuals become alienated, the normal pronouncements of "law and order" fall on deaf ears. Law requires a consensual society, in order to be functional. Where that consensus has broken down, the most important first step is to search for a new consensus, a new basis for unity. The harsh imposition of law, made by an old order, which many consider illegitimate, will lead not to *political* rule, but to military government.

America has to come to terms with the hard implications of massive alienation. This country can no longer assume the existence of a consensus. This country is faced with a serious crisis of authority, a most serious crisis of legitimacy. The problem cannot be understood simply in terms of a small group of people running wild, having fun, and wreaking havoc because there is nothing better to do.

Relevant intermediary groups. In *The Politics of Mass Society* William Kornhauser suggests that one way to guard against conditions of mass anomie, chaos, and violence is to make sure that the masses of people have meaningful groups to which they can relate. People do not blow up or burn down those things (including their neighborhoods) in which they feel they have a stake. And the mechanism is to create organizations which legitimately claim the allegiance of people. These organizations can then proceed to involve the membership in relevant, constructive activity that points toward building society, not tearing it down.

The 29th Ward on the west side of Chicago vividly illustrates this point. That ward is well over 90 per cent black, with a total population of nearly 77,000 people. This is one of the areas that exploded in violent rioting in April 1968 after the assassination of Dr. Martin Luther King, Jr. In the 29th Ward of Chicago, the life of most black people is bleak and depressing. Many Americans did not understand then—and still do not—the frustration of these people. But to whom could the blacks turn? The Democratic ward committeeman is white and, according to reliable reports, does not live in the area. At least half of the 58 precinct captains are white and, similarly, are non-residents of the community. The black people there simply feel no kinship to that structure. It is not relevant in their lives. It is not functional *for them.* The 29th Ward is a politically illegitimate situation *vis à vis* the black people who live there. Therefore, black people must move to establish their own relevant intermediary groups, more frequently than not, Black Power-oriented.

Unfortunately, much of white America has assumed that

the institutions and organizations it has created to rule over black America are relevant to the latter. It is becoming clear that such is not the case. And as black people have come to express their rejection of the *status quo*, and as they have moved to set up relevant intermediary groups, they have been accused of being black racists and segregationists. The fact is, however, that such new groups are probably the first step toward creating a viable society.

Political modernization. Societies that are undergoing change and development are constantly involved in three on-going processes: centralization, a search for new values and new forms of decision making, and broadening the base of political participation. These three processes can be observed, for example, in the breakup of feudalism, moving into monarchic government on the European continent and into parliamentary government in England. I suggest that we are witnessing these processes today in this country, particularly as we focus on racial problems. Indeed, this country is underdeveloped; it is in the process of modernizing. This country has its people coming out from under colonial rule.

Few persons would deny that the demands of the black community have played an extremely important role in the centralization of power in the United States. Clearly, more power is being accumulated in the federal government. Since the turn of the century, and especially since the New Deal, black Americans have looked to the central government for the resolution of their problems. Today many mayors are calling on the federal government to do more to help solve what has come to be called the "urban crisis." Recent demands for "community control" at first glance appear to be a move toward decentralization. But, on closer examination, one finds that many of the "community con-

trol" groups are seeking, in fact, to create new relationships
with the federal government. Thus, this move is not to be
equated to the basically anticentrist stance of conservatives
and of white, Southern segregationists (the States Righters),
who likewise advocate local, community control. The blacks
who make these demands are looking for ways to devise
new structures which will be legitimately responsive to
people and which will ensure that the resources available
at the federal level will find their way down to those who
need them the most. This may call for a re-examination of
the roles of many city halls, county court-houses, and state
capitols. If those places of power are not performing legitimately, they should not be retained. This is the very hard
kind of thinking and re-examining that needs to be done.

It is important to note, as does David Apter in *The
Politics of Modernization*, that when we speak of legitimacy
we are speaking normatively first, and structurally second.
In other words, before we can proceed to ask and answer
questions concerning political legitimacy, we must focus
first on the normative values of the society. A society which
is modernizing is constantly re-examining its normative
values, as well as searching for new forms of decision-
making; and any society which stops questioning its values
and stops re-examining its forms of decision-making is
likely to be a society that has started on the route toward
decline and decay.

I believe that black people have performed a most useful
function for the country by raising new, hard questions
which challenge the presumed validity of many of the norms
and institutions of the society. It is painful to many, perhaps, to hear the country labeled as "racist," but this permits the society to re-examine itself. Admittedly, the
atmosphere is filled with emotion and contentiousness and
animosity, but the process of social change, more frequently

than not, is traumatic and unpredictable. The country now has the opportunity to take a long, hard look at its institutions and to search for ways to revise them. This modernizing process has been absent from the American scene, especially since the end of World War II and the coming of the Cold War. When one views the problem in this manner, one might correctly conclude that black Americans have, indeed, been in the *avant-garde* of those modernizing America. Black people, therefore, can be seen as men and women of modernity. This proposition might sound arrogant and presumptuous, but it is set forth seriously.

When one talks of America and of bringing more people into the political process in the past thirty years, one must, of necessity, focus on the efforts of black Americans. In conjunction with the federal agencies—the courts, the Congress, the executive, as opposed to the state and local authorities—black people have steadily fought to break down barriers to political involvement. Now, with the Black Power movement, they are politicizing increasingly large numbers of people. Black people are becoming more and more involved and are demanding not only an equitable distribution of goods and services, but also an equitable distribution of decision-making power.

In this context, I am suggesting that Black Power, as a political phenomenon, addresses itself to the problem of alienation and the need for relevant intermediary groups, and that it is an essential part of the modernizing process of the centralization, the search for new values and new forms, and the constant broadening of the political base.

II

There are many programs under way in black communities across the country which illustrate the attempt to work

out the problems described above, such as the establishment of economic co-ops similar to the Grand Marie Co-op
in Opelousas, Louisiana, where black farmers (growers of
cabbage, sweet potatoes, and okra) pool their resources and
market co-operatively. Buying clubs and credit unions have
developed from this venture, which was started in 1966 by
CORE (the Congress of Racial Equality) with a membership originally 20 per cent white, but which today is all
black. There is also Operation Breadbasket, with head-
quarters in Chicago, which organizes black people to boycott those merchants and manufacturers in the black communities who fail to hire significant numbers of black
persons, and who fail to stock the products of black manufacturers. This endeavor is successful in negotiating and
bargaining, and there is the realization that there is an
organizable potential for power in the buying ability of
blacks. Branches are being established from coast to coast.

We can point to the many "relevant intermediary groups"
developing in the black community—teachers, social workers, policemen, professionals, labor-union workers. There
is the Association of Afro-American Educators, a national
group of black teachers, which is determined to teach black
children in black-ghetto schools in a manner that has meaning for them. Those teachers are saying that they will not
be agents for the transmission of an irrelevant white culture but will see that the curricula reflect black experiences,
black history, and black culture. In line with this, we
see the development of many "Concerned Black Parents"
groups, calling for community control, because they no
longer have faith in many of the city boards of education
or in the many white-dominated P.T.A.'s. One can understand this phenomenon, also, in the emergence of many
black college and high school groups. These students are
requiring their schools to revise their curricula to be more
relevant, to be more reflective of the pluralistic, hetero-

geneous nature of the society. Probably one of the most important relationships to develop out of this will be that between the newly sensitized black teachers and the black students. It is quite possible that a wholly new and healthy learning environment will be created. This, as most know who are familiar with conditions in the black ghetto schools, will be an innovation of major proportions.

It is not accidental or insignificant that black policemen in Chicago, New York, and Detroit have formed Afro-American Patrolmen's leagues, saying, in essence, that they will be the protectors of the black community, not its persecutors. They understand that the traditional role of the police in the black communities has been to maintain order with very little, if any, emphasis on justice. They hope to change that. They hope to instill a sense of trust and confidence in the police on the part of the black citizens, and they are aware that the role of the police, vis-à-vis those citizens, must change.

In some cities, black people are starting corporations, hiring blacks, selling shares in the corporations to the employees, permitting them to become part owners, and developing at least some economic independence. We see this with the N.E.G.R.O. (National Economic Growth and Reconstruction Organization) in New York. The group has purchased a hospital, a textile-manufacturing company, a chemical company, and a bus company. The leaders feel an intense sense of responsibility to help develop viable bases of economic power in the black community.

One cannot overlook the movement among black workers in various labor unions such as D.R.U.M. (Dodge Revolutionary Union Movement), or the Concerned Transit Workers in Chicago, demanding that those unions (which have enjoyed an image of liberalism and egalitarianism) begin immediately to share decision-making power with the black members. In all too many of those locals, the black worker has been simply a dues-paying member who has seldom been in the inner councils. Again, the black people are saying: not just goods and services, but decision-making power.

In the area of electoral politics, we observe a growing awareness among black spokesmen that candidates for public office (black as well as white) must begin to address themselves, in a meaningful way, to the needs of their black constituencies. Thus, in the 1968 Presidential campaign, the National Committee of Inquiry was formed to interview the Presidential candidates to discern their views on issues of primary importance to black Americans. That committee is also concerned with the composition of important congressional committees—that is, committees handling bills important to the immediate and long-term interests of black people.

As more black people move into the cities, and as their level of political consciousness and sophistication grows, we shall see the election of more men such as Richard Hatcher and Carl Stokes as mayors. Their election will not be a panacea (any more than is the election of any official), but they will undoubtedly be able to relate to many black people more easily than some of their predecessors. At least, it is unlikely that they will be as insensitive and indifferent to blacks as many of the men who have previously occupied city halls. In addition, these black mayors can go to Washington for help and speak with authority. They are probably not out of touch with the intense needs of the black communities. Whether they will be listened to by the decision-makers in the federal government, of course, depends on a number of things out of their control. But the beginning of a constructive equation for social change is there. It is still an open question whether the country is wise enough to work with these kinds of legitimate leaders.

III

Finally, we must briefly consider violence, so often connected with Black Power in the popular press, within the conceptual framework of this essay. (I am not going to discuss the violence heaped upon black people by whites, but, rather, two forms of violence relevant for the black community.) A distinction between two types of violence, expressive violence and instrumental violence, needs to be made. Expressive violence is what we have experienced in this country since July 1964, when masses of people explode out of frustration and rage in a flurry of looting and destruction of property. Such expressive violence waxes and wanes, depending as much on the weather as on anything else (and often takes on an atmosphere of fun and frolic). But expressive violence must be contrasted with instrumental violence, which does not burn a random liquor- or furniture-store, but destroys a communications system. It is not casual sniping at policemen and firemen, but selective retaliation. Instrumental violence does not wax and wane with the weather, but builds sanctuaries of support in the black community, or, in other parts of the world, in the village. This is guerrilla warfare; and it is highly disciplined. The United States is, clearly, one of the luckiest of countries in having the kind of massive oppression which exists, and only expressive violence. However, as the society procrastinates in dealing with the causes of expressive violence, it will surely have to come to terms with instrumental violence.

Black Power need not be connected at all with either expressive or instrumental violence, although it speaks to the alienation, institutional illegitimacy, and political backwardness which breed violence. The subject of this essay has been sociopolitical legitimacy, because *that* is what Black Power is about. It seeks to overcome alienation; it seeks to establish relevant intermediary groups for black Americans; it seeks to lead this country along a path of political modernization.

My ultimate goal is a Just and Open Society. This is the goal of the Black Power I advocate. America today is *not* a Just society; it is *not* an Open society. America today is a racist, oppressive, backward society. The Black Power I discuss is the beginning of an alternative to that condition. It is important that the reader understand this presentation as a developmental model.

As we develop theories, chart courses, formulate plans, organize groups, many of us can only hope that America will be as wise as she is wealthy.

Epilogue: A Dream Deferred

The subtitle of this collection of essays, "Reflections on the Negro Experience in America," suggests an occasion for evaluating the significance of this experience for our society. For the black American, such an examination offers an opportunity to explore his place in history, a place long denied him. For white Americans, it represents opportunity to begin, as Otey Scruggs notes, "to become familiar with a past that has been far from exclusively white." The reaction of contemporary blacks to the "Negro experience in America" has been one of distrust. Why? To understand this attitude, whites must consider how they might react to such an experience.

The history of the black man in America has been a chronicle of frustration. Joseph Logsdon describes the slaves' yearning for freedom and their response to what they believed to be their deliverance by Yankee troops. "Freedom was the slaves' goal. . . . That dream never came true. The Yankee 'liberators' thrust them back to the soil, to the white man's soil as free laborers. . . . They [the army leaders] did not come to free men. . . . Liberation was an afterthought." James McPherson shows that the opportunities provided by Reconstruction raised the hopes of the freedmen. However, he notes, the "period of bright promise in the late 1860s . . . flickered in the backlash of the 1870s." In Booker T. Washington's lifetime, it was believed that if the Negro would only pattern his life after the Bookerite model, he would gradually be accepted to equal and full status in American society. This strategy, so admired by white Americans, failed. Negroes discovered that this strategy was, as Louis Harlan shows, "unable to change the course of the dark river of racial intolerance." The "promised land" of the North provided only further degradation and frustration.

These and other experiences litter the path of the black American from 1619 to the present. Such experiences do not engender trust, but rather distrust, frustration, and anger—*Black Rage*, as Grier and Cobbs put it. After so many promises, the black American is cautious about raising his hopes again. Past promises have been empty. Why, he asks, should those that are currently extended lead to any different experience from those of the past?

"Integration" best describes what white America currently offers the black American. It is the promise of equal status and full participation in American society. "Until very recently," writes James Barnes, "most black Americans have been staunch adherents of integration, and many continue to cling to this vision of society. It is, however," he warns, "a vision that many have rejected, and many others have begun to doubt."

The rejection of integration by black Americans is due to a growing suspicion, engendered by the general white reaction to efforts at desegregation, that real integration is impossible. Such resistance characterizes the white response in both the North and the South, and is a major obstacle to the black man's achieving equal status in American society. Furthermore, white Americans have also resisted efforts to provide, through education and training, the means by which the black American can prepare himself to accept a full role in American society.

Why has white America failed to fulfill the promise? One reason is that public support for freedom and full citizen status for black Americans has not gone beyond passing laws or handing down new legal decisions. Legislation is often viewed as the end, rather than as an early step in a social process involving the interplay of two obstacles to full citizenship. One obstacle arises from white attitudes and their influence in shaping the institutions which sustain and perpetuate the situation in which the black American lives. The other obstacle is the socio-psychological results of inferior, restricted status and general degradation which have, until now, characterized the life of black Americans.

The relationship between white attitudes and the manner in which black Americans function as members of our society is described by Myrdal:

> . . . the White majority group . . . naturally determines the Negro's place. All our attempts to reach scientific explanations of why they live as they do have regularly led to determinants on the white side of the racial line. In the practical and political struggles of effecting changes, the views and attitudes of the white Americans are . . . strategic. The Negro's entire life, and consequently, also his opinions on the Negro problem, are, in the main, to be considered as secondary reactions to more primary pressures from the side of the dominant white majority.

White Americans generally have refused to acknowledge this relationship between their attitudes and the lives of black Americans. The result has been an inability to understand the problem and, consequently, an inability to take appropriate corrective measures. Indeed, the will to correct the problem often appears to be lacking in white Americans. An illustration of such a failure of will is found in the Reconstruction era. Although Constitutional amendments were passed to provide to the freedmen their "rights," according to James McPherson, Reconstruction failed to achieve full status for the freedmen because a "genuine revolution of equality would have required a revolution in institutions and attitudes which did not occur." However, as McPherson notes, "the illiteracy, inexperience and poverty of the freedman" also contributed to the failure. There is still this double obstacle to black equality, to the black man's full participation in our society.

For most black Americans, there has been no opportunity for integration. For others who have lived and worked with whites, integration has not proved to be *the* resolution to racial conflict. We have often assumed that, once integration was achieved, mutual respect would follow automatically, as if we needed only to place a black child and a white child, a black family and a white family, a black employee and a white employee, side by side to obtain the desired consequences.

The expected results have not necessarily followed. The black child in the "integrated" school is often the object of white children's derision. The black family in the "integrated" neighborhood may be ostracized or overly cultivated, but natural relationships with white families in the neighborhood seldom result. The black employee in a management position is placed in a showcase and used to demonstrate both compliance with the law and his employer's liberalism, but he often has lunch alone and generally moves in isolation from those with whom he is "integrated."

"Integration" has demanded that blacks adjust to, and master, the demands of school, work, and family-living in a complex, specialized society from which they have previously been excluded. The "integrated" black has found that he must be an ideal student, family member, or employee, that he must verge on sainthood to be a "credit to his race." He must also accept the role of "educator of whites," while withstanding and accepting his own frustration, if not indignation, at whites' insensitivity and lack of understanding of the black man in America.

The black person (or family) in the "integrated" situation resents being the "token," being the resident—whether in job, school, or neighborhood—representative of his "race," being the local authority on all issues pertaining to Negroes. He resents such an emphasis on his blackness, because it reflects stereotyping in a new disguise. The implication is that all black men are alike. Whichever black man is available is a suitable representative of his race.

Blacks who live and work in integrated situations are also faced continually with whites' protestations and efforts to demonstrate their tolerance and understanding. In spite of their professed understanding, such people are usually oblivious to blacks' hostile reaction to being "tolerated and understood" by whites who are obviously uncomfortable with them.

To be "integrated" with whites, the black American must withstand such pressures and, at the same time, effectively live, work, study, and play. While he may appear to do so, many blacks are pushed to the breaking point. Grier and Cobbs describe such an instance:

A black man, a professional, had been a "nice guy" all his life. He was a hard-working non-militant who avoided discussions of race with his white colleagues. He smiled if their comments were harsh and remained unresponsive to racist statements. Lately he has experienced almost uncontrollable anger toward his white co-workers, and although he still manages to keep his feelings to himself, he confides that blacks and whites have been lying to each other. There is hatred and violence between them and he feels trapped. He too fears for himself if his control should slip.

The only result that "integration" can guarantee is social proximity. Such proximity is valuable only to the extent that communication, an exchange of information, occurs; proximity without communication may have little influence on persons' prejudices and outlooks. Although proximity existed in the ante-bellum South, the thoughts and feelings of slaves reflected in their diaries, as Joseph Logsdon points out, contradict the description of slaves and slavery written by whites.

To avoid a comparable lack of understanding today, whites who seek out, or accept, participation in an integrated situation must realize that they have only begun the process of transcending the indoctrination regarding blacks that American society imposes on its white citizens. Old stereotypes, and inadequate or erroneous information, must be corrected; and the general discomfort at associating with blacks on an equal basis must be overcome. Such changes take place only with concerted effort. For many, the cost is too great.

In their study *Interracial Housing*, Morton Deutsch and Mary Evans Collins show that living next door to a Negro family does not necessarily produce changes in attitudes. These authors compared the attitudes of women living in integrated housing, whose attitudes changed, with those of women in the same situation whose attitudes did not change:

When they [those whose attitudes changed] moved into the project, though typically prejudiced, they were relatively young and comparatively better educated. As a consequence of casual experiences in school or in factories during the war Negroes were not completely strange to them. Placed in a situation where contact with Negroes was almost inevitable, they had more flexibility and experience with which to make an adaptation. To live with Negroes as next door neighbors presented, furthermore, less of a status threat because they pictured themselves as being "working class" rather than "middle class." Adapting themselves to their Negro neighbors instead of withdrawing and cutting themselves off brought closer contact with Negroes, and with closer contact prejudices were shed. As a consequence of their friendly relations with the Negro people, they faced many problems in relation to the prejudiced broader community. Sharing these problems with their White neighbors, they were drawn closer to them and came to know them and like them better than women who had cut themselves off from relations with the Negro people.

In contrast, the housewives who [because of age, lack of education, or middle-class identification] lacked the flexibility to adapt to intimate social contacts with Negroes were relatively uncomfortable in the integrated projects. By cutting themselves off from the Negro people, they were led also to limit their social relations with the other white people in the project in order to avoid embarrassing situations and the social presures toward conformity to the social norms of the project. As a result the ratios of their outside friends to friends within the project were higher than those of the housewives who changed in attitudes.

"Integration" provides only the *opportunity* for changing one's attitudes. Whether or not one actually changes is due both to his own personal make-up and to how he uses the opportunity before him. If he fails to meet and develop friendships with his black neighbors in an integrated situation, changes in attitude are unlikely.

To develop a natural relationship between blacks and whites in an integrated society requires examination of the complex motivation which influences individuals in such situations. For example, some whites are involved in interracial activities principally to assuage their guilt. Regardless of the reason for the guilt itself, such a purpose for participating in interracial activities is destructive. It is simply another instance of whites' using the black man for their own psychological ends. Malcolm X, in his autobiography, speaks to this point:

I have these very deep feelings that white people who want to join black organizations are really just taking the escapist way to salve their consciences. By visibly hovering near us, they are "proving" that they are "with us." But the hard truth is this isn't helping to solve America's racist problem.

Activities which appear to represent self-sacrifice on behalf of the improvement of the status of blacks may, on closer examination, be seen to perpetuate the idea that the black man is inferior. Whites have tended to want to run black organizations, to secure the black man's civil rights, and, generally, to improve his "lot." Such attitudes, apparently vestiges either of paternalism or of Calvinistic moralism, give rise to the expectation that blacks will accept what is handed them, "stay in their place," and "love" the ones who did all these things for them. Many blacks have done just this, but increasingly their "Uncle Tom" response is being rejected. Black Americans see that this type of black-white relationship simply perpetuates inferior status. Rather than making it possible for the black man to gain or maintain his self-respect, white control fosters dependency, undermining the black's self-respect and his efforts to take a full and responsible place in society.

Instances in which whites resist blacks' taking responsibility for their own affairs and those of the black community emphasize the tendency to perpetuate inferior status. When blacks do take responsibility, whites often feel rejected or angry or insist on "how much they have done for the Negro." The feeling of loss and rejection, rather than the feeling of pride and satisfaction at the achievement which taking responsibility implies, reflects the whites' *need* for the *status quo*. Such a need may involve assuaging guilt or simply resistance to changing old perspectives. But whites should not be surprised that their participation in interracial activities is rejected when it means the subversion of black efforts to achieve a responsible status in American society.

In fact, Malcolm X questioned all white participation in black organizations.

I mean nothing against any sincere whites when I say that as members of black organizations, generally whites' very presence subtly renders the black organization automatically less effective. Even the best white members will slow down the Negroes' discovery of what they need to do, and particularly of what they can do—for themselves, working by themselves, among their own kind, in their own communities.

The well-intentioned efforts of whites may perpetuate the image of black inferiority in other ways. Even efforts to "help" the black man may conspire to perpetuate the feeling of inferiority of which James Baldwin speaks:

... every Negro child knows what his circumstances are though he can't articulate them, because he is born into a republic which assures him in as many ways as it knows how ... that he has a certain place and he can never rise above it.

This image of inferiority is sustained in various ways by our educational system, by the ghetto, by segregated neighborhoods, even by the welfare system.

The "help" provided by public assistance is the last resort for those, white as well as black, whose resources, not only financial, but usually physical, mental, and social, have declined to such a degree that they become eligible for it. Once a person is eligible, the system seems to focus on keeping him that way. Too little attention is given to methods to reverse this destruction of human resources. Adults who need help to regain their place as self-sustaining citizens are seldom given such help; and, as a result, dependency and inferiority are perpetuated.

Black Americans have responded to the continuing imposition of inferior status with the concept of Black Power. As Charles V. Hamilton notes, there are many definitions of Black Power, but the most significant implication of all of them is that blacks are working to remove the marks of centuries of inferior status, demanding to do for themselves, to act in their own behalf. Blacks are saying to whites: "Help us help ourselves! Give us 'technical assistance.' Use your skills to help us do those things we set out to do; teach and train, but do it with the realization that where the activities are in behalf of blacks, you will be directed by black administrators and citizens' groups. Don't try to take things over and make them your own. In such activities, the final responsibility is ours."

Black Power aims to end the perpetuation of inferior status by the education system, by employment practices, and by housing restrictions. Quite simply, if whites, either on their own or in cooperation with blacks, will not, or cannot, cease the practices which support ideas of racial inferiority, blacks must act themselves.

Does Black Power mean the end to integration as a goal? Yes, if by integration is meant the "tokenism" that has so far characterized integration. Yes, if white Americans generally continue their resistance to more than token integration. Yes, if integration is to continue to imply superiority for whites and inferiority for blacks.

Black Power can be a perspective from which blacks can relate to whites so that each contributes to the society of which both are equal parts. Black Power can be the base from which blacks can be respected by whites and whites can be trusted by blacks. Black Power can be the process by which the place of black Americans in American society is no longer disparaged, but becomes a source of pride to both black and white Americans.

Selective Bibliography

I: General Histories

The best introduction to the history of the Negro in the United States is John Hope Franklin, *From Slavery to Freedom** (1969, rev. ed.). Although it was written as a textbook, its style is lucid and its scholarship sound. E. Franklin Frazier, *The Negro in the United States* (1949), takes a more sociological approach and remains extremely useful. Earl E. Thorpe, *The Mind of the Negro: An Intellectual History of Afro-Americans* (1961), makes useful beginnings in the area of intellectual history on which all of these books are weak. Excellent, briefer, studies are those of August Meier and Elliott M. Rudwick, *From Plantation to Ghetto: An Interpretive History of American Negroes** (1966); and Benjamin Quarles, *The Negro in the Making of America** (1964). *Before the Mayflower: The History of the Negro in America, 1619–1966** (1966), by the *Ebony* editor Lerone Bennett, Jr., lacks the balance of a general history but makes exciting reading, as does J. Saunders Redding, *They Came in Chains** (reissued 1968). Recently, two excellent documentary histories have appeared: Leslie H. Fishel, Jr., and Benjamin Quarles, eds., *The Negro American: A Documentary Story** (1967); and Gilbert Osofsky, ed., *The Burden of Race: A Documentary History of Negro-White Relations in America** (1969). These supplement but do not replace Herbert Aptheker, ed., *A Documentary History of the Negro People in the United States*, 2 vols. (Vol. I, 1962; Vol. II, 1964), which carries the story to 1910. Changing white attitudes are the subject of David Reimers, *White Protestantism and the Negro* (1965), and Thomas F. Gossett, *Race: The History of an Idea in America** (1963).

* Available in paperback.

II: *Slavery*

The best general study of slavery is Kenneth M. Stampp, *The Peculiar Institution** (1956). Stampp thoroughly revises the earlier work of Ulrich B. Phillips, *American Negro Slavery** (1968 ed.). Certain of Stampp's theses are in turn challenged by Stanley Elkins, *Slavery** (1969, rev. ed.). This controversial book draws heavily on Frank Tannenbaum, *Slave and Citizen** (1947), for a comparative view of slavery in the Americas.

Various aspects of the slave trade are treated in: Basil Davidson, *Black Mother: The Years of the African Slave Trade** (1961); Eric Williams, *Capitalism and Slavery** (1944); W. E. B. DuBois, *Suppression of the African Slave Trade to the United States, 1638–1870** (1898); and Frederick Bancroft, *Slave Trading in the Old South* (1931).

The origin of slavery in the English mainland colonies is debated in: Oscar and Mary F. Handlin, "Origins of the Southern Labor System," *William and Mary Quarterly*, VII (April 1950); Carl N. Degler, "Slavery and the Genesis of American Race Prejudice," *Comparative Studies in Society and History*, II (October 1959); and Winthrop D. Jordan, "Modern Tensions and the Origins of American Slavery," *Journal of Southern History*, XXVIII (February 1962). Lorenzo J. Greene, *The Negro in Colonial New England** (1942), is a good monograph on that area; while Robert McColley, *Slavery and Jeffersonian Virginia* (1964), serves to dispel several myths about the economy of that area and the attitudes of the Founding Fathers. Herbert Aptheker, *Nat Turner's Slave Rebellion** (1968), and *American Negro Slave Revolts** (1943), are the most extensive studies of these subjects. Eugene D. Genovese, *The Political Economy of Slavery** (1965), is a series of provocative essays. Richard C. Wade, *Slavery in the Cities: The South** (1964), treats a hitherto unstudied subject in a superb fashion.

An increasing number of slave narratives are being reprinted in modern editions. Joseph Logsdon and Sue Eakin have done

* Available in paperback.

a fine job of editing Solomon Northup's *Twelve Years a Slave* (1968), and more recently Gilbert Osofsky has edited three of the best known slave journals in a single volume, *Puttin On Ol Massa** (1969).

David B. Davis, *The Problem of Slavery in Western Culture* (1966), and Winthrop D. Jordan, *White Over Black: American Attitudes Toward the Negro, 1550–1812** (1968), are two brilliant studies dealing in detail with white attitudes toward Negroes and slavery in the cultural and psychological context of the seventeenth and eighteenth centuries.

III: *The Civil War and Reconstruction*

Leon Litwack, *North of Slavery** (1961), is an exceptional book on the condition and activities of Northern Negroes before the Civil War. The two best histories of the abolition movement are Dwight L. Dumond, *Antislavery: The Crusade for Freedom in America** (1961); and Louis Filler, *The Crusade Against Slavery, 1830–1860** (1960). On the place of Negroes in the antislavery movement, they must be supplemented by: Benjamin Quarles, *Black Abolitionists* (1969); Herbert Aptheker, *The Negro in the Abolitionist Movement** (1941); and Larry Gara's excellent study of the underground railroad, *The Liberty Line** (1967). The greatest of the black abolitionists, who later was a leader of the Republican Party, is the subject of Benjamin Quarles, *Frederick Douglass** (1948). Philip Foner, ed., *Life and Writings of Frederick Douglass** (1950–1955), is excellent, particularly on Douglass's postwar career. Both Douglass's *Narrative of the Life of Frederick Douglass** and *The Life and Times of Frederick Douglass** are available in recent editions and should not be ignored.

The performance of Negro soldiers during the Civil War is treated in Benjamin Quarles, *The Negro in the Civil War** (1953), and Dudley T. Cornish, *The Sable Arm: Negro Troops in the Union Army, 1861–1865** (1956). Bell I. Wiley,

* Available in paperback.

Southern Negroes, 1861–1865* (1965), adequately covers the subject. James M. McPherson, *The Negro's Civil War** (1965), is a vivid documentary history.

The recent literature on Reconstruction has almost completely revised the general view of that period. Kenneth M. Stampp, *The Era of Reconstruction, 1865–1877** (1965), and John Hope Franklin, *Reconstruction: After the Civil War** (1961), are syntheses of the most recent scholarship. James M. McPherson, *The Struggle for Equality: Abolitionists and the Negro in the Civil War and Reconstruction** (1964), is an excellent study. W. E. B. DuBois, *Black Reconstruction in America** (1935), remains the only synthetic study of Southern Negroes during Reconstruction. It should be supplemented by Vernon L. Wharton's model study, *The Negro in Mississippi, 1865–1890** (1947); Joel Williamson, *After Slavery: The Negro in South Carolina During Reconstruction** (1965); and Joe M. Richardson, *The Negro in the Reconstruction of Florida, 1865–1877* (1966). Unfortunately, the pioneering work of A. A. Taylor, with the exception of the material in the *Journal of Negro History* in the 1920s and 1930s, is generally unavailable. Seth M. Scheiner, ed., *Reconstruction: A Tragic Era?** (1968), is a good introduction to the various interpretations of the period.

White attitudes toward Negroes during these years are covered in: William R. Stanton, *The Leopard's Spots: Scientific Attitudes Toward Race in America, 1815–1859** (1960); Eugene H. Berwanger, *The Frontier Against Slavery* (1967); V. Jacque Voegeli, *Free but Not Equal* (1967); and Forrest G. Wood, *The Black Scare* (1968).

IV: *The Age of Booker T. Washington*

A general study of the years at the end of the nineteenth century is Rayford W. Logan, *The Negro in American Life and Thought: The Nadir, 1877–1901** (1954). Although it covers many other topics, C. Vann Woodward, *Origins of the New*

* Available in paperback.

South, 1877–1913* (1951), provides an excellent introduction to the context within which Washington operated Woodward's interpretation of the origins of segregation is further developed in his fine brief volume, *The Strange Career of Jim Crow** (1966, rev. ed.). This should be supplemented by a series of state studies: Vernon L. Wharton, *The Negro in Mississippi, 1865–1890** (1947); George B. Tindall, *South Carolina Negroes, 1877–1900** (1952); Clarence Bacote, "Negro Proscriptions, Protests and Proposed Solutions in Georgia, 1880–1908," *Journal of Southern History*, XXV (November 1959); Charles E. Wynes, *Race Relations in Virginia, 1870–1902* (1961); and Frenise Logan, *The Negro in North Carolina, 1876–1894* (1964). An excellent contemporary discussion is Ray Stannard Baker, *Following the Color Line: American Negro Citizenship in the Progressive Era** (1908, reissued 1964). Joel Williamson has put together relevant materials from contemporaries and historians in *The Origins of Segregation** (1968).

Guion G. Johnson, "The Ideology of White Supremacy," in Fletcher M. Green, ed., *Essays in Southern History* (1949), and Idus A. Newby, *Jim Crow's Defense: Anti-Negro Thought in America, 1900–1930* (1965), analyze the defense of segregation. Louis R. Harlan, *Separate and Unequal: Public School Campaigns and Racism in the Southern Seaboard States, 1901–1915* (1968), is an excellent study which illuminates much more than the single issue with which it is concerned.

The literature on Washington is voluminous, but of limited scholarly usefulness. An exception is August Meier's fine book, *Negro Thought in America, 1880–1915** (1963), which presents the most sophisticated analysis of Washington's thought, such as it was. Samuel R. Spencer, Jr., *Booker T. Washington and the Negro's Place in American Life** (1955), is a brief, readable, but overly laudatory introduction to Washington's life. Two good studies of Washington's major opponent for racial leadership are: Francis L. Broderick, *W. E. B. DuBois: Negro Leader in a Time of Crisis* (1959); and Elliott M. Rudwick, *W. E. B. DuBois: A Study in Minority Group Leadership*

* Available in paperback.

(1961). No student should fail to read the self-evaluations of these great men: Booker T. Washington, *Up From Slavery** (1901); and W. E. B. DuBois's essays, *Souls of Black Folk** (1903), and autobiography, *Dusk at Dawn: An Essay Toward an Autobiography of a Race Concept** (1940). Hugh Hawkins, ed., *Booker T. Washington and His Critics** (1962) is a helpful introduction to the subject.

V: *Urbanization*

The migration of blacks to the cities is covered generally in: Arna Bontemps and Jack Conroy, *Anyplace but Here* (original title: *They Seek a City*) (1966); and Reynolds Farley, "The Urbanization of Negroes in the United States," *Journal of Social History*, I (Spring 1968). Karl E. and Alma F. Taeuber, *Negroes in Cities* (1963), describes patterns of segregation and movement in the cities.

The rise of the ghetto has been the subject of a number of recent studies dealing with the early years of this century. Unfortunately, no study exists to complement W. E. B. DuBois's pioneering *The Philadelphia Negro: A Social Study** (1899). Seth M. Scheiner, *Negro Mecca** (1965), and Gilbert Osofsky, *Harlem: The Making of a Ghetto** (1966), treat the development of the New York black community before 1930. Two older books on Harlem by leaders of the Harlem Renaissance are: James Weldon Johnson, *Black Manhattan* (1930; 1968*); and Claude McKay, *Harlem: Negro Metropolis* (1940). Roi Ottley, *New World A-Coming* (1943), is a journalistic account of Harlem during the Depression. Harold Cruse, *The Crisis of the Negro Intellectual** (1967), is a brilliant and unique work that is essentially an intellectual history of Harlem. John Henrick Clarke, ed., *Harlem: A Community in Transition* (1965), originally appeared in *Freedomways*. Allan H. Spear covers the early period for Chicago in *Black Chicago* (1967), and provides an introduction for the classic study by Horace Cayton and St. Clair Drake, *Black Metropolis* (1945). Kenneth Clark,

---

* Available in paperback.

Dark Ghetto* (1965), is a penetrating recent study of the ghetto subculture by a leading black social psychologist; and Robert C. Weaver's older book, *Negro Ghetto* (1948), remains useful.

The literature on black institutions is limited. The controversial report of Daniel Patrick Moynihan, *The Negro Family: The Case for National Action** (1965), has been issued in a paperback edition which includes much of the commentary on the report, *The Moynihan Report and the Politics of Controversy** (1967), edited by Lee Rainwater and William L. Yancey. There is no adequate study of the urbanization of the Negro church, but W. E. B. DuBois, ed., *The Negro Church* (1903); Benjamin E. Mays and Joseph W. Nicholson, *The Negro's Church* (1933); Carter Woodson, *History of the Negro Church* (1921); Arthur Huff Fauset, *Black Gods of the Metropolis: Negro Religious Cults of the Urban North* (1944); and E. Franklin Frazier, *The Negro Church in America* (1964), are all useful, particularly the Frazier book. E. David Cronon, *Black Moses: The Story of Marcus Garvey and the Universal Negro Improvement Association** (1955), is the only scholarly biography of that important figure. Amy Jacques Garvey (the wife of Marcus Garvey) edited *Philosophy and Opinions of Marcus Garvey* (1923). E. U. Essien-Udom, *Black Nationalism: A Search for an Identity in America** (1962), is the best study of that subject, but it should be supplemented with C. Eric Lincoln, *The Black Muslims in America** (1961). James Baldwin's novel *Go Tell It on the Mountain** (1954) evokes the ethos of the store-front church.

The best books on Negro urban politics deal with Chicago. Harold F. Gosnell, *Negro Politicians: The Rise of Negro Politics in Chicago* (1935), is an excellent pioneering study, while James Q. Wilson, *Negro Politics: The Search for Leadership** (1960), brings the story through the 1950s in superb fashion. Nathan Glazer and Daniel Patrick Moynihan, *Beyond the Melting Pot: The Negroes, Puerto Ricans, Jews, Italians and Irish of New York City** (1963), places the Negro in the

* Available in paperback.

broad context of New York ethnic politics. The rise of Carl
Stokes in Cleveland politics is the subject of Kenneth G. Wein-
berg's *Black Victory* (1968). Harry Bailey, ed., *Negro Politics
in America** (1967), is a collection of excellent recent essays.

VI: *Protest Movements*

Lerone Bennett, Jr., *Confrontation: Black and White** (1965),
is a general history of Negro protest. Francis L. Broderick and
August Meier, eds., *Negro Protest Thought in the Twentieth
Century* (1965), is a documentary history with a useful introduction.

There is no adequate history of the most prominent activist
civil rights organization, the National Associaton for the Advancement of Colored People (NAACP). Robert L. Jack,
*History of the National Association for the Advancement of
Colored People* (1943), sketches the early years of the organization. Langston Hughes, *Fight for Freedom: The Story of the
NAACP* (1962), is a popular account. At present Charles
Flint Kellogg is writing a scholarly history of the organization,
but only the first volume, *NAACP: A History of the National
Association for the Advancement of Colored People, 1909–
1920* (1967), has appeared.

The Rev. Martin Luther King, Jr., led the Southern Christian Leadership Conference (SCLC) to prominence after the
Montgomery bus boycott. King described the events in Montgomery in *Stride Toward Freedom* (1958), and developed his
philosophy of nonviolence more fully in *Why We Can't Wait*
(1964). L. D. Reddick, *Crusader Without Violence* (1959),
and Lerone Bennett, Jr., *What Manner of Man: A Biography
of Martin Luther King, Jr., 1929–1968* (1968), are biogra-
phies of Dr. King. A somewhat more sophisticated analysis is
August Meier, "On the Role of Martin Luther King," *New
Politics*, IV (Winter 1965). Louis E. Lomax, *The Negro Revolt** (1962), reviews and criticizes this phase of the movement, particularly the nonviolent philosophy.

* Available in paperback.

After the Montgomery experience came the sit-ins and the freedom rides, which increased support for the new direct-action organizations: The Congress of Racial Equality (CORE) and the Student Nonviolent Coordinating Committee (SNCC). These movements are treated in James Peck, *Freedom Ride* (1962), and Howard Zinn, *SNCC: The New Abolitionists* (1964). The effect of these groups on an older organization, the Urban League, is seen in Whitney M. Young, Jr., *To Be Equal** (1964); whereas the former leader of CORE and one of the most articulate of black spokesmen, James Farmer, explains the growing militancy of the movement in *Freedom— When?** (1965).

Black Power has emerged from the reappraisal of the nonviolent philosophy. This phenomenon is best explained in Stokely Carmichael and Charles V. Hamilton, *Black Power: The Politics of Liberation in America** (1967), and Lewis M. Killian, *The Impossible Revolution: Black Power and the American Dream** (1968). Two points of view on Black Power are given in David Danzig, "In Defense of Black Power," and Bayard Rustin, "Black Power and Coalition Politics," both in *Commentary*, September 1966.

The forces for black equality are best identified by the men who represent them. The recent autobiographical and semi-autobiographical literature is exceptionally rich. Many black authors have portrayed the Negro American, but few have done so with the power and artistic grace of Richard Wright in *Native Son** (1940) and *Black Boy** (1945), and Ralph Ellison, *Invisible Man** (1952). More recently, James Baldwin has had a powerful influence through his essays, collected in three books: *Nobody Knows My Name** (1954); *Notes of a Native Son** (1955); and *The Fire Next Time** (1963), which reflects the sentiments behind the black man's inclinations to violence. Claude Brown, *Manchild in the Promised Land** (1965), describes growing up in Harlem. Malcolm X, *The Autobiography of Malcolm X** (1964), occupies an important place in contemporary black thinking and is an extraordinary

* Available in paperback.

social document. Eldridge Cleaver, *Soul On Ice* (1968), presents the perspective on Black Power of a leader of the militant Black Panthers.

VII: *Sociological and Psychological Perspectives*

Contemporary examinations of the sociology and psychology of Negro-white relations begin with Gunnar Myrdal, *The American Dilemma** (1944), a monumental, if now somewhat dated, study of the different aspects of race relations in the United States. Oliver C. Cox, *Caste, Class and Race* (1948), stresses the economic dimension in racial prejudice and questions Myrdal's view that black-white relations in America are primarily determined by American social structure. There are several good collections of relatively technical papers on minority-majority relations. Two of the best-balanced in terms of coverage of different topics are Bernard E. Segal, ed., *Racial and Ethnic Relations** (1966); and Raymond W. Mack, ed., *Race, Class and Power* (1963). Peter I. Rose, *They and We** (1964), is a short introduction to research and theory in intergroup relations, though its scope does not approach that of Gordon W. Allport, *The Nature of Prejudice** (1954), which considers the major theories of prejudice and research on the topic. George E. Simpson and J. Milton Yinger, *Racial and Cultural Minorities* (1965), provides more up-to-date findings and a good review of perspectives on prejudice and discrimination and on the social and economic position of the Negro. The influence of segregated and interracial housing on prejudice has received considerable study. Morton Deutsch and Mary E. Collins, *Interracial Housing* (1951), is a good example of this type of work. Robin M. Williams, Jr., *Strangers Next Door* (1964), is a more recent study of prejudice and its influence on racial residential patterns. Leonard Broom and Norval Glenn, *Transformations of the Negro American* (1965), analyzes the position of the Negro in American society with particular consideration given to his occupation and income.

* Available in paperback.

Pierre L. van den Berghe, *Race and Racism* (1967), is an interesting cross-cultural examination of racism and provides an important dimension to historical considerations of the topic. The socio-psychological characteristics of black Americans are described in Myrdal. Thomas Pettitgrew, *A Profile of the Negro American* (1964), is a more recent work on the topic. There have also been a number of important studies of the psychological and social effect of prejudice and inferior status, particularly in the South. Among these are John Dollard, *Caste and Class in a Southern Town** (1937); Allison Davis, B. B. Gardner, and M. R. Gardner, *Deep South* (1941); and Abram Kardiner and Lionel Ovesey, *The Mark of Oppression* (1951). William H. Grier and Price M. Cobbs, *Black Rage** (1969), is somewhat fragmented but interesting for its case studies, as is Robert Conot, *Rivers of Blood, Years of Darkness** (1967), which focuses on selected participants in the 1965 Los Angeles (Watts) riot.

Charles Silberman, *Crisis in Black and White** (1964), is a good introduction to the contemporary crisis in race relations. Michael Harrington, *The Other America* (1962), deals with the problem of Negro poverty. Nat Hentoff, *The New Equality** (1964), examines the economic and social changes prerequisite to achieving black equality.

John P. Davis, ed., *The American Negro Reference Book* (1965), is an encyclopedic volume of essays covering nearly all aspects of "the Negro experience in America."

* Available in paperback.

Contributors

JAMES F. BARNES, assistant professor of political science at Ohio University, was born in Petersburg, Virginia. He was educated at Ohio State University. In 1963 and 1964 he served on the Ohio Legislative Service Commission, and from 1965 to 1967 was a member of the United States delegation to the North Atlantic Treaty Organization. He is a specialist in urban politics. His published works include *Representation and Reapportionment: The Case of Ohio* (1964) (in collaboration with others) and a number of papers done for the Ohio Legislative Service Commission.

CHARLES V. HAMILTON, Ford Professor of Political Science at Columbia University, is an expert on contemporary political systems and Southern politics as well as the problems of the urban ghetto. He was born in Muskogee, Oklahoma, and educated in Chicago at Roosevelt University, Loyola University, and the University of Chicago. Professor Hamilton's published works include *Minority Politics in Black Belt Alabama* (1965); *The Politics of Civil Rights* (1967); and, with Stokely Carmichael, *Black Power: The Politics of Liberation in America* (1967). Professor Hamilton served as a consultant to NBC News for their series "The Urban Crisis in America" and is working on a book tentatively entitled *Black Americans and Political Modernization*.

LOUIS R. HARLAN, professor of history at the University of Maryland, is editor of the Booker T. Washington Papers, a multivolume project aided by the National Endowment for the Humanities and the National Historical Publications Commission. Born in Clay County, Mississippi, in 1922, he was educated at Emory University, Vanderbilt University, and the Johns Hopkins University. Professor Harlan is a specialist in Negro and Southern history. His published works include *Separate and Unequal: Public School Campaigns and Racism in the Southern Seaboard States, 1901–1915* (1958) and *The Negro in American History* (1965). Professor Harlan is currently completing research for a biography of Booker T. Washington.

ROY C. HERRENKOHL is associate professor of social psychology and methodology at Lehigh University. Born in Huntington, West Virginia, he was educated at Washington and Lee College, the University of Reading (England), Union Theological Seminary, and New York University. A specialist on social attitudes and social motivation, Professor Herrenkohl is also consultant to a project on attitude measurement at the New York University Research Center for Mental Health.

JOSEPH LOGSDON, associate professor of history at Lehigh University, was born in Chicago. He was educated at the University of Chicago and the University of Wisconsin. He is a specialist in Negro history and nineteenth-century United States history. His publications include *Horace White: Nineteenth Century Liberal* (1970) and a new annotated edition of Solomon Northup, *Twelve Years a Slave* (1968). Professor Logsdon is currently editing a new edition of Albert T. Morgan, *Yazoo: Or the Picket Line for Freedom in Mississippi* (1884), and working on a history of the New Orleans Negro community.

JAMES M. McPHERSON, associate professor of history at Princeton University, was born in Valley City, North Dakota. He was educated at Gustavus Adolphus College and the Johns Hopkins University. He is a specialist in abolition and Reconstruction, as well as Negro history. His publications include *The Struggle for Equality: Abolitionists and the Negro in the*

Civil War and Reconstruction (1964), which won the Anisfield-Wolf Award in race relations; *The Negro's Civil War* (1965); *Marching Toward Freedom: The Negro in the Civil War* (1968); and "The Antislavery Legacy: From Reconstruction to the NAACP," in Barton Bernstein, ed., *Towards a New Past: Dissenting Essays in American History* (1968). Professor Mc-Pherson is currently working on the postwar response of abolitionists and their families to the plight of the Negro.

SETH M. SCHEINER, associate professor of history at Rutgers University, was born and educated in New York City and received his degrees from City College of New York and New York University. Professor Scheiner is a specialist in Negro and urban history. His publications include *Negro Mecca: A History of the Negro in New York City, 1865–1920* (1965); *Reconstruction: A Tragic Era?* (1968); and a pamphlet prepared for the Philadelphia public school system, "Guide to the History of the Negro American." He is currently at work on a study of Philadelphia during the Progressive period.

OTEY M. SCRUGGS, professor of history at Syracuse University, was born in Vallejo, California. He was educated at the University of California at Santa Barbara and at Harvard University. He is a specialist in labor history and Negro history. Professor Scruggs's publications include (with Peter H. Merkl) *Rassenfrage und Rechtsradikalismus in den USA* (The Race Question and Right-Wing Politics in the U.S.A.) (Berlin, 1966). Professor Scruggs is currently working on a biography of Alexander Crummell, a nineteenth-century Negro clergyman and intellectual leader who founded the American Negro Academy, the predecessor of the Association for the Study of Negro Life and History.

WILLIAM G. SHADE, associate professor of history at Lehigh University and editor of *Pennsylvania History*, was born in

Detroit, Michigan, and educated at Brown University and Wayne State University. He is a specialist in the political history of nineteenth-century America and is the author of several articles, including "The Radical Republicans: An Essay Review," *Pennsylvania History, XXXVI* (July 1969). He has also edited and contributed to *Lawrence Henry Gipson: Four Dimensions* (1969).

Index

Note: Asterisk (*) indicates entry is in footnote.